THE INVESTMENT TRAIN:
Choosing the Right Track to Retirement

By Joseph V. Curatolo

ISBN 0-9719830-0-3

9 780971 983007 >

Covers by Tim Vogel. The Amtrak Acela illustration is used with written permission of the National Railroad Passenger Corporation and Amtrak®.

Printed in Canada

To my wife Kathy for twenty years of encouragement, wisdom and support. Your attention to detail amazes me and your outlook on life inspires me everyday.

And to my parents Rocco and Terry, you not only taught me a strong work ethic and real family values, you live your teachings every day.

Acknowledgments

Over the years I've learned that no one becomes successful by himself. I've been blessed to have an invaluable support team. Thank you to the entire staff at Georgetown Capital Group, especially Stacey Pempsell, Erin Cleary, and Diane Johnson. We have the best staff that anyone could put together, and I admire your relentless desire to improve the services we provide to our clients.

Without hesitation, I must acknowledge my fellow financial planners at Georgetown Capital, especially Ron Migliore, Steve Wzontek, Mike Curatolo, Ed Harof, Dan Martin, and Tim Geidel. We've worked together in some cases twenty-two years, and I appreciate sharing the same rewards and frustrations on a daily basis.

I have to thank some of the many investment professionals I've enjoyed working with over the past twenty-six years, including: Mark Goldberg, Hy Cohen, Gary Krat, Jim Tambone, Steve Gibson, and Kevin Myeroff. They represent some of the best people in the business, and I'm proud to work with them.

A special thank you for my media consultant, Steve Reszka. He has delivered more value to our firm than we could have imagined. Steve has worked on this book with me from the beginning and brought together all the talents to get the job done. In that same vein, thank you to Carol Anne Wilson and Tim Vogel, without whom we never could have done this book.

Finally, special thanks to Philomena Mattera, whose wisdom has taught me more about life and responsibility than anyone can realize.

Contents

Preface

Time is one of our most valuable resources. And thankfully, due to advances in technology, medicine and investment opportunities over the last thirty-plus years, we now have more time to spend well beyond our 60s, or "in retirement."

More than 75 million Americans are 50 years of age or older. These folks will live, on average, longer than their parents. Many are looking for ways to get more out of life by working smarter, not harder. To some, that means leaving the workforce sometime after the age of 50. For others, it may mean starting a new career. And still other "retirees" are planning a total change of lifestyle. In order to satisfy those goals, you need to work smart to get more out of your financial plan.

And expectations are high! We baby boomers have seen a lot of changes in the world since our high school days. Computers are the norm and many people wouldn't be caught dead without their mobile phones! We've seen the "dot-coms" come and go, the deregulation of several businesses, and most of all, have gained the knowledge and experience that only comes with passing time. Your life and all the things in it are much more multifaceted and complex than family life was for your parents.

And unlike our parents, it's becoming clearer we likely will not be able to depend upon Social Security as the primary "salary" to carry us securely through our golden years. Even with pensions and other savings plans, the changing complexion of the financial world has complicated things – it's the rare person who can just begin taking money out of his or her retirement accounts without professional guidance.

It's probably a good bet that if you're reading this book, you are not a Gen-Xer or Generation Y member looking for retirement information. There are several basic advice books for 20 and 30-year olds and people looking for a good financial base plan. This book is written for you, the 40 to 60-year old retirement-objective worker. You already are working smarter, not harder. My audience for this book likely has a retirement plan, or at least an objective. You're looking for some assistance in the best ways to invest, withdraw and maintain your current standard of living when you retire.

I'm often asked during seminars or national radio interviews for investment advice. While some advice can be applied generally, most people need individual attention to focus on their risks, tolerances and future desires, and how that mix becomes a retirement portfolio.

Georgetown Capital Group clients know that we work hard to provide personal, professional service. Some of them have agreed to allow their investment stories to be used as examples of how to retire smarter, not harder.

We strive to show individuals, families, and businesses how to accumulate wealth, now and for your future. I thank those of you who already are GCG clients and know we keep our promises. To others who are considering joining Georgetown Capital Group, I think this book will be of great assistance to you. We're ready to build a comprehensive, custom-tailored financial plan designed to give you what you need – now and in the future.

Joseph V. Curatolo
Williamsville, NY
May 2003

Chapter 1:

Determining What You Need

Laying Down the Tracks

Retirement no longer conjures up the image of an elderly person working on crossword or jigsaw puzzles to while away the time. Retirement means an active, healthy lifestyle – someone enjoying life and getting the most out of it after putting in time and making investments to get you there.

If you are over 40 years of age or close to 50, it's time to really assess where you're going and just how you're going to finance your retirement.

I've worked with hundreds of investors, most doing quite well now in retirement. But it doesn't come about magically – for some folks, my brand of retirement won't come about at all! My clients are the savers – the people who have taken control of their lives, put aside some money (and received company funds as well), and are ready to take a realistic look at just how much they'll need to continue living at their current income level. No unrealistic dreams here, just the secure knowledge that they will be able to live in the style to which they've become accustomed for the rest of their lives. Not too bad a deal!

Where to start? The most important place is with a financial advisor. You need someone who is working in the field day by day, someone who is up on the constantly changing laws and market influences and can use that knowledge to assist you in getting the most bang for your bucks. (We'll discuss the many advantages of professional advice in Chapter 5.)

In the next several chapters, we'll examine how to assess your investments, what changes may need to be made to your portfolio and how much money you'll need to retire. In Chapter 2, we'll discuss how best to gather and prepare your information. In Chapter 3, several means are used to determine just how much money you'll need in retirement. Chapter 4 determines your risk tolerance. Then, in Chapter 5, we'll look at how to reallocate your assets for the best mix. Chapter 6 discusses professional advice versus do-it-yourself; Chapter 7 is an overview of insurance. In Chapter 8, we'll examine some common problems and how to avoid them. Chapter 9 deals with taxes, while Chapter 10 looks at estate planning and gifting.

The Good Life

Remember the old Tony Bennett song, "The Good Life"? He sings, "Oh the good life, full of fun seems to be the ideal... it's the good life to be free and explore the unknown…" Isn't this what we want from retirement? To live the "good life" without the worries of how to earn your next dollar?

It can happen, if you plan well and receive good advice. In fact, you can retire prior to age 62, even prior to age 59. Most of my clients have done so and continue to increase their principal and dividends, as long as the markets allow.

A recent American Association of Retired Persons (AARP) survey finds baby boomers are independent and self-reliant when it comes to retirement income. As a matter of fact, some baby boomers anticipate (and look forward to) working part-time to supplement any retirement income. In the 1998 publication, *Baby Boomers Look toward Retirement*, Roper Starch Worldwide reports boomers have two simple responses when it comes to what they associate with the word retirement: having enough money and financial security.

Let's look at how one couple has ensured financial security and is looking toward a "good life" which allows them to continue along as they are – financially secure.

James and Kelly* (names have been changed to respect privacy) are retired. James is 56 and Kelly is 52. James worked for 30 years for a large communications corporation and saved $400,000 in his 401(k) and received a $400,000 lump sum pension. Kelly worked part-time while raising their family and her paychecks contributed to savings and IRAs. So, James and Kelly have about $200,000 invested in mutual funds and personal IRAs as well.

Before retirement, James brought home a paycheck of about $3,500 a month – that's after taxes. And now James is retired, continuing to collect that same amount of money and maintain his standard of living. Our objective in retirement is to replace your disposable income from wages and possibly add cost of living raises.

After a thorough review of his 401(k) and pension fund, we created two separate IRAs for James. One receives the pension in a lump sum; the other is a growth IRA. These funds allow James to take advantage of certain tax codes (we will discuss those codes, including Rule 72T, in greater detail in a later chapter), maximizing the amount of money available.

James and Kelly know they'll need about $42,000 a year after taxes to live comfortably. Their portfolio needs to be right around where it is – in the $600,000 to $1,000,000 range. Your financial advisor can help you determine if your withdrawal rate is realistic and at what age retirement is most feasible. You may need to consider increasing how much you're putting into your portfolio or even adjust your risk tolerance level.

When Do I Start Planning?

"If only I had started sooner!" That's one of the most frequent comments I hear when discussing retirement. I even hear it when I appear on radio talk shows.

In our discussions on retirement, one thing rings clearly — it's never too early to get on the investment track. Saving at any age is good. However, it's also extremely important to know when to seek professional advice. Often, when you're younger, errors and lack of in-depth knowledge may lead your portfolio astray. Then, by age 50, it's not as easy to get things back on track. That's why I want you to start out on the right track now! By evaluating your retirement options prior to age 50, you can work to set up a comfortable plan such as the one serving James and Kelly.

It's also wise to find a financial advisor who will not only counsel you and advise you as to the best investment strategies for your situation, but someone who has a wealth of experience and resources available to determine the greatest investment strategies.

Taking the First Step

Get out your paycheck stubs, your credit card statements, all the records that will help you determine how much you're currently spending. Will those expenses change significantly after retirement?

Think about your hobbies and activities. You'll have more time now to enjoy golfing, fishing, perhaps home remodeling, and even buying more things for your grandchildren. What about medical coverage? Will you have to pay more out of pocket in retirement? And what about travel? Are you planning to take more trips? All this adds to your bottom line.

How about expenses that will decrease, such as commuting costs? Perhaps you can use just one car now. And how about dry cleaning expenses, or uniform costs – those will be significantly reduced, if not gone.

Many retirement planning books recommend a base of about 60 to 80 percent of your after tax dollars earned for your retirement income. I strenuously disagree! This is important, because it means the difference between a comfortable retirement and one in which you're trying to pinch pennies. You need the same amount of income after retirement that you were earning while working. The objective here is to replace your current disposable income so you can maintain your style of living.

Remember, retirement can last 30 or 40 years! Can you live comfortably on 5% or 6% of your portfolio? That's our objective here. Most retirees live off of about 7% to 10% of their retirement portfolio. Also, you need to think about any added expenses during retirement. Will you possibly need additional health care? What about nursing home costs? These are things that should be built into your retirement plan.

A Quick Review

- Can you retire early and do well, regardless of whether it's your choice or if you're forced into it through your employer? Do you have a good framework in place? Do you have a financial advisor?
- Are you ready to determine what it is you'd like to do in retirement and map out a plan? Can you preliminarily determine what some post-retirement expenses may be?
- Are you considering retirement investments with long-term benefits? Because we are living longer and are healthier than previous generations, we need to carefully consider retirement investments to get the most out of our dollars.
- Do you know all the tax reduction tools at your disposal that allow you to retain as much of your money as possible? Have you asked your financial advisor?

Chapter 2:

Adding Up What You Have

How Many Boxcars Are On This Train?

Think of all the times you've gotten in your car, ready to take a trip. You're certain the gas tank is full, but when you check you discover there's just a quarter tank of gasoline, not nearly enough to get you to your final destination. While it's not too difficult to drive to the nearest gas station to fill up, in retirement, thinking your portfolio is "full" only to discover a quarter of a tank could spell disaster! It's time to crunch some numbers! Simply put, do you have enough saved to retire? Is your gas tank full?

I read about a very sad case a few months ago. A newspaper in Texas reported a story about a woman who completely misunderstood retirement and Social Security. For this 67-year old widow, retirement was a rude awakening! She admitted to a newspaper reporter, "I didn't think about it. When you're young, you think you're going to be young forever." Now, this woman must work just to keep her household afloat. She receives a retirement check of about $300 along with Social Security benefits of about $200 a month. Her job pays about $14,000 a year, and this woman told the reporter she now expects she never will be able to retire. How heartbreaking!

While I certainly hope none of you reading this book would ever find yourselves in such dire straits, the story raises a very important point when it comes to retirement planning. Not only is it something to think about— right now— but without proper guidance, you may be fooling yourself into believing you'll be set when the time comes.

It's very easy to underestimate just how much you need after you've stopped working. That's what we'll do in this chapter – take a look at your assets, all the money you have saved, including investments and retirement plans, and calculate if you're set for your golden years.

Here's a little warning: if in your 60s you have $300,000 or $400,000 set aside in various accounts earmarked for your retirement, you may not be able to retire as early as James, whom I discussed in the last chapter. But in your 40s or 50s, with a concrete plan to save toward retirement, you may be able to look toward ending your work years sooner than your peers.

We begin by getting organized and reviewing your investments. Is your money outpacing inflation? If not, you may run out of retirement funds.

It can seem overwhelming to try to look at the future with an eye toward retirement. Again, I can't say this enough – this is where dealing with your financial advisor is invaluable. He or she can make this review well worth the investment of time and money.

Checking Out Your Nest Egg

You need to start by getting organized and preparing to make a plan. Gather all your investment documents and statements. Review your portfolio. Take a good long look at everything you own. Ask yourself some hard questions, such as, "What is my investment style?" I ask all my clients this question: "If you had the chance to start from scratch and re-do your current portfolio, would you reacquire everything you own now?" If the answer is no, I ask them why they still own that stock or fund!

Check everything in your portfolio and ask the hard questions: Am I emotionally attached to this stock? Am I duplicating efforts? Am I proud that I bought this, or embarrassed? How often have I gotten burned?

By doing this, you are forced to take a good look at everything you own and why you own it. For example, if you have two mutual funds and one is doing much better than the other, why not consolidate and invest in the fund with better growth? However, watch for overlap. It's extremely important for you to keep track of how much you own of any one stock. Your financial advisor can best show you how to check your funds' shareholder reports to log all your stock holdings.

Another important part of assessing your portfolio is to create a risk tolerance profile. This helps you determine just how much money you want to keep at certain risk levels, and allows your financial planner to create a portfolio with the maximum return for your level of risk. You'll find a risk tolerance profile later in this book.

It's likely there will be a need to shift some things around in your retirement plan, especially if you have been investing without professional advice. Once you're comfortable with your revised portfolio, it's time to examine the type of lifestyle you want in retirement. Remember, the goal is to match your current disposable income so you can maintain your standard of living. If you're in a field where you receive a lot of overtime pay, instead of matching your base salary, it's prudent to average your paychecks over the last six months and use that figure for your monthly income base.

Reviewing the Basics

It seems there's a veritable number and alphabet soup out there when it comes to retirement plans and options – 401(k), 403(b), IRA, etc. Let's take a quick review of what is available.

401(k) and 403(b)

We'll begin by looking at retirement plans offered by your employer, generally known as qualified plans. Somewhere in the neighborhood of 65% of Americans are offered a retirement plan, for example a 401(k) or a 403(b). The names of these plans come from tax codes. If your company has one of these plans available, be certain to participate! Enrollment is well worth the time and effort.

In a 401(k) plan, your employer takes pre-tax salary, and possibly after-tax money, and puts it in a tax-deferred account. Often, employers may match your contributions perhaps 50 cents on the dollar, or even dollar for dollar through company stock. You decide where your money is invested. One caveat though: it's very important to understand your stock options.

A 403(b) plan is very similar and is offered to people working for educational institutions and non-profit companies. Sometimes there are greater restrictions of 403(b) plans, and some colleges and universities set a cap on employees' contributions. If you work for a non-profit organization, be certain to check with your employer to determine if there are limits on the amount you contribute.

401(k) savings plans are fast becoming a leading source of retirement funds for many workers. Yet, research from Charles Schwab shows about 20 percent of eligible workers just don't contribute at all, or do not contribute enough to reap the most rewards from their 401(k) plan.

Another problem centers on workers who, when they change jobs, opt to cash out their 401(k) accounts and spend the proceeds rather than move the funds to their new employer's 401(k) plan, or roll it into an IRA.

And even if you do invest in your 401(k) plan at work, sometimes the people selecting the plan's investment choices don't have the depth of financial knowledge needed to make smart decisions. Some plans are filled with high-fee mutual funds or annuities with poor results, or very few investment choices.

Retirement Plan Contribution Limit Increases

Year	401(k) & 403(b)	401(k) & 403(b) for those 50+
2001	$10,500	$10,500
2002	$11,000	$12,000
2003	$12,000	$14,000
2004	$13,000	$16,000
2005	$14,000	$18,000
2006	$15,000	$20,000
2007	$15,000	$20,000
2008	$15,000	$20,000

Other Pitfalls

What are some other problems? By far, the leading problem for employees is underestimating the value of matching funds from your employer. A 401(k) plan provides you the opportunity to build a retirement fund using what is close to being free money. Your employer may provide some percentage of matching funds to contributions you make to your 401(k). That adds up to extra contributions for you, which when compounded over several years can contribute to a healthy bottom line.

Another pitfall involves owning too much of your company's stock. Taking advantage of an opportunity to purchase stock at a discount coupled with matching 401(k) funds may make you a great cheerleader for your company, but it also could leave you with some big holes if times get tough.

When the Enron Corporation's stock collapsed, many workers had overloaded their 401(k) accounts with Enron stock. The debacle not only wiped out retirement plans for many people, but it has put 401(k) reform at the top of the agenda for Congress. But recent news reports indicate 401(k) deficiencies won't be ironed out any time soon. This is one more important reason why having a qualified, knowledgeable financial planner is so important.

Your portfolio may contain much more of your company's stock than you think, and that could put you at risk. Your financial advisor is qualified to assist you in ensuring your 401(k) plan is doing what it is supposed to do – help make money!

I also personally call and meet my clients throughout the year to discuss their portfolios and determine if their investment train needs to change tracks or make slight adjustments. It's never a static course, and I always make myself available to give my clients the advice and time necessary to keep things "rolling down the track."

Cash Balance Plans

Recently, some companies have begun moving toward using cash balance plans in favor of traditional pensions. Usually, pensions are determined by a formula taking into account your years of service with the company and your salary as you near retirement. A cash balance plan is similar to a profit sharing plan. It credits your pension account with a percentage of your current pay, with the company guaranteeing the contributions will grow by a certain percentage annually.

In the last five to ten years a number of large corporations have been offering their rank and file employees the ability to take the traditional annuity pension versus a new cash balance (lump sum) system. In other words, the employee could take a pension check every month for the rest of his or her life, or a lump sum dollar amount that should provide the same amount of income as the annuity pension would.

For a traditional monthly pension, corporations might make available to a retiree $2,000 a month for the rest of his or her life. Should he or she die, the family receives nothing after that. In most cases, these plans also offer a slightly reduced monthly pension should the employee wish to take a survivor option. In this particular case, the employee would take a 10% reduction in their pension and if they pass away, their spouse would receive half for the rest of their life.

In the example that we spoke of earlier, a retiree would either take $2,000 a month for the rest of his or her life with nothing after that for their surviving spouse, or take a 10% reduction of $2,000 each month or $1,800 a month for the rest of his or her life. When the employee passes away the spouse would be entitled to one-half of the $1,800 or $900 a month. This is generally known as the 50% survivor option. In some cases, if the spouse were to predecease or pass away before the retired employee, then the retired employee would "pop up" back to their original pension, which would be $2,000 a month in our case example.

When these options are available, the employee and their spouse must sign off on them and it is considered irrevocable; they cannot change it once they start it. If someone were to take a 50% survivor option and become divorced from their spouse, they cannot change their pension calculation.

In the above example, a company would come up with a "cash balance plan" where the corporation would say, *You have the opportunity to take the $2,000 monthly income for the rest of your life or reduced amount for you and your spouse or, hypothetically $350,000 in a lump sum pension— you take it, roll it over in an IRA in your name, and life goes on.* This employee pension benefit has nothing to do with any other benefit that the retiree would have such as medical benefits or life insurance.

In this particular case a retiree would have to analyze the benefits of taking a $350,000 lump sum cash buy-out of his or her pension, and determine if he or she could invest it, receive hypothetically $2,000 a month which in essence is about a 6.8% distribution rate from the $350,000 lump sum dollar amount.

The benefit of the cash balance plan is that the money is in the employee's name, in his or her estate, and if something were to happen and he or she passes away or his or her spouse passes away, then it goes on to the heirs.

There is a tremendous benefit here for anyone looking for the cash balance plan. Something to take into consideration here is, do you believe you could generate the income that would match the $2,000 a month in our illustration? What's your health like? Do people in your family generally live to be one hundred years old? In that particular case, the monthly annuity for the rest of your life may be a better option, or is your health not the best? Have you had three bypass surgeries in the last two years? In that particular case, the cash balance plan may be a strong contender as your option to take the money and run and have the money in your family name.

You'll have to name your beneficiaries, which could be your spouse, your children, your grandchildren, possibly even a trust account that could be set up to dispense money to your wife, children, grandchildren, heirs, etc. We call this "strings from the grave" because you can have a variety of features and restrictions as to how the beneficiaries would get the money. In some cases it might be a staggered benefit: your children may not get the money until they are age 30, 35 or 40 or something like that.

The cash balance plan is becoming more and more popular in large corporate pension plans, and it's something that the majority of the retirees are taking—taking the money, investing it wisely. One of the other things that you have to consider is if you are a spendthrift, you may spend the money aggressively and blow through it within hypothetically ten or fifteen years, which is obviously dramatically shorter than your own life expectancy. These are some of the things that you have to wrestle with, and possibly have a few sleepless nights in determining what your own present state of mind would be.

Individual Retirement Accounts (IRA)

Even if you have a retirement plan with your company, you can establish your own IRA. In a traditional IRA, you can contribute up to $3,000 in 2002. That tax-deferred money grows until you withdraw it, which you can do after age 59½. However, there is a way to withdraw IRA funds early, prior to age 59½, without penalty.

A Roth IRA is more flexible than a traditional IRA. Eligibility depends upon your income. Roth IRAs are designed for single investors with incomes less than $100,000, or married investors with a combined income of less than $160,000.

The government created IRAs about twenty years ago as an incentive for the American taxpayer to save for the future. The government and Congress knew that Social Security may not be the best thing out there, or may not be available to everyone in its current format. They believed there had to be some sort of an incentive for Americans to save for the future but penalize them if they were to invade the principal. So the government started the old familiar $2,000-a-year IRA, which most people took advantage of to save for the future.

As everyone knows, you put money away into an IRA and you take it out later on when you're retired after age 59½. If you were to take out money before age 59½, there would be a 10% penalty. The logic there is that the penalty is being invoked because you're not using the money with its original intent. The original intent was for these monies to be there for your retirement, and for some reason they came up with the time frame of age 59½.

Later in the book we will talk about two ways to get your money out of your tax deferred account without the 10% penalty.

Contribution Limits

Year	IRA Contribution Limit	IRA Add'l Contribution 50+
2002	$3,000	$500
2003	$3,000	$500
2004	$4,000	$500
2005	$4,000	$500
2006	$4,000	$1,000
2007	$4,000	$1,000
2008	$5,000	$1,000
2009	$5,000*	$1,000
2010	$5,000*	$1,000

Indexed for inflation in $500 increments

SEP, EIRA and ESOP

It sounds like alphabet soup, but each plan is designed for specific circumstances. A SEP is a Simplified Employee Pension, an alternative for people who are self-employed or who may own a small business with few employees. SEP plans allow you to contribute up to 15% or $24,000 of your income, whichever is less. Withdrawal rules are the same as for traditional IRAs.

An EIRA is an Educational IRA, a trust or custodial account you fund to help contribute to education expenses of a designated beneficiary. That beneficiary could be your child, grandchild, or another minor. If you establish the EIRA, you manage the EIRA— the beneficiary does not. The amount of money you contribute to the EIRA is not tax deductible, but it does grow tax-free until distribution. Additionally, the beneficiary will not owe taxes on withdrawals if the qualified educational expenses for the year equal or exceed that amount. However, if your salary is over a certain limit, you cannot create an EIRA. (Parents and grandparents may also be interested in a new educational savings plan known as a 529 plan. We'll discuss the details in a later chapter.)

Some things to know about an EIRA:

- *The Educational IRA may be used for elementary, secondary or college education. Effective January 1, 2002, income is capped at $110,000 for a single parent and $220,000 for married couples, up from $95,000 to $190,000 respectively.*
- *Contributions will be raised to $2,000 per year from $500 effective January 1, 2002.*
- *Withdrawals are free from federal income taxes as long as they are used to cover qualified education expenses. Effective January 1, 2002, qualified withdrawals will include tuition, fees, academic tutoring, books, supplies, room and board, uniforms, transportation, computer technology and equipment for kindergarten through college.*
- *Withdrawals used for non-qualifying expenses are subject to income tax and a 10% penalty.*
- *Once the beneficiary reaches age 18, no additional contributions may be made. There are other limits on contributions, which you should discuss with your financial advisor.*

If the beneficiary reaches age 30 and there are still funds in his or her Educational IRA, the funds must either be distributed (incurring tax or penalty) or rolled over to benefit another family member.

ESOP stands for Employee Stock Ownership Plan, and allows you to acquire your company's stock. Not a bad plan if you have lots of faith in your company. However, it means all your retirement funds will be in just one company! For some workers recently, that's spelled disaster (remember Enron). So, if you have an ESOP through work, plan on investing in other types of retirement funds, such as IRAs to help diversify your portfolio.

Other Areas to Review

Okay, you've checked out your retirement accounts. Now, you'll need to gather information about any mutual funds, stock, bonds, money market, or CD accounts. Also, you'll want to include any savings accounts you have. Do you own any other valuables? Perhaps land or jewelry? Only include those items as assets *if* you're considering selling them in the future.

Insurance is another important issue. Check out whether or not your company provides health insurance during retirement. Also consider auto insurance, homeowner's policies and life insurance and how much you're spending on each. What's the value of your life insurance? We'll get into insurance and the pluses and minuses in an upcoming chapter.

Purchasing Power

Remember, it's not just the income you're earning today. Inflation is the ruin of us all – we need purchasing power in our retirement portfolios. Purchasing power doesn't come from savings accounts. Your financial advisor can assist you in setting up a retirement savings plan with several components to help your money earn the most it can before you stop working.

Often, mutual funds, stocks and bonds yield the greatest returns for retirement planning, but many investors find it difficult to determine the correct mix of stocks to bonds to IRA funds to CDs, etc.

The recent roller coaster-like ups and downs of the stock market have some folks feeling a bit queasy about keeping a higher percentage of savings in stocks. Take Mark, a 54-year-old teacher, for example. He's reducing his stock allocation in his retirement portfolio from 80 percent to 50 percent. A younger teacher, Ross, says at 38 he'll stay the course with about 85 percent of his retirement portfolio in stocks, since he's not retiring for another 20 years or so.

Here's a quick quiz for you:

Would you invest in the stock market today if you knew:

- *The Prime Rate would reach 20 percent?*
- *Home mortgage rates would rise to 18 percent?*
- *Bankruptcies and bank failures would reach an all-time high?*
- *The stock market would fall more than 20 percent in one day?*
- *The price of oil would reach nearly $40 a barrel?*
- *The president would be shot?*
- *The U.S. would be involved in a war in the Middle East?*
- *Rioting would return to the streets of Los Angeles?*
- *The U.S. would be victim to international terrorism?*
- *Real estate values would drop as much as 30 percent?*

Interestingly enough, it's all happened. If you had money invested in the stock market from 1981 to 2001, you would have earned an annual rate of return of 10.95% in the S&P 500 Index. That's better than any savings account. However, it's critical to state that achieving these results is best done with the assistance of a financial advisor who devotes each working day to following the ups and downs of the financial world.

ANNUAL RETURNS FOR S&P 500
$10,000 Investment as of January 1, 1981

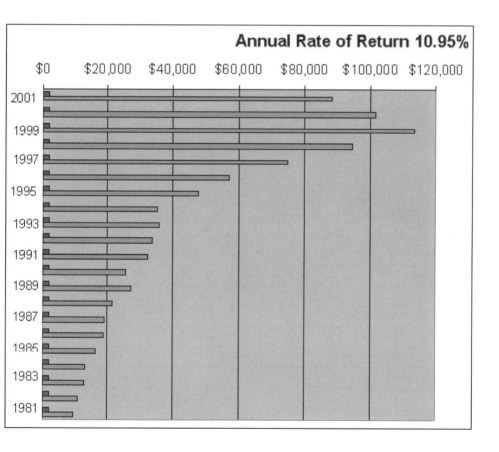

Crunch Time

Georgetown Capital Group clients are familiar with the process we call Asset Allocation Modeling. It's where we check to see just where your assets are. With this worksheet, you'll be able to determine if your retirement savings are on track.

Asset Allocation Modeling
Where are your assets (excluding your home)?

Type of Asset	Dollars, Bank Deposits or Bonds	Stock or Growth	Other
Total of Assets	$	$	$
Percentage of Allocation	%	%	%

Hypothetical Asset Allocation

Type of Asset	Dollars, Bank Deposits or Bonds	Stock or Growth	Other
Cash Balance Plan	300,000		
401(k)		100,000	
IRA	50,000	100,000	
Bank & Credit Union	10,000		
Series E Bonds	10,000		
Individual Stocks		50,000	10,000
Total	370,000	250,000	10,000
Total of Assets	$630,00	$500,000	$20,000
Percentage of Allocation	59%	39%	2%

In the illustration above, our client has about 60% of his investment assets in cash or bonds and about 40% in equities for growth. This mix is on the conservative ide of asset allocation.

One asset not included on the modeling chart is your home. Still, it is a good ime to determine if you plan to stay in your current home or if you'll be making a nove and downsizing. Remember, moving costs money, too!

Taking a look at your assets helps you determine if your funds are working est for you. It's a matter of considering all the options. You need to ask yourself ome serious questions – are you comfortable with the percentage of funds in the tock market? Your 401(k)? Your asset allocation is something you and your inancial planner should review every year. Your skilled advisor is much more likely o be up on any new choices or changes in the market. It's the best way to assist ou in determining the best mix of stocks, bonds, and cash.

A Quick Review

- It's never too early to think about investing for your retirement. When is the last time you reviewed your retirement plan? Have you examined the amount of money you're putting in each year? The interest you're receiving?
- Do you, or have you considered seeking professional advice when it comes to determining the right mix of investments?
- Are you taking full advantage of the many ways to help your retirement portfolio, including 401(k) or other employer-assisted plans?
- If you change jobs, will you make certain you don't cash out your 401(k)?
- Did you diversify your portfolio?
- Do you know the difference between a pension plan and a cash balance plan?
- What do you know about IRAs?
- Are you comfortable with stocks?

Chapter 3:

Estimating How Much You Need

You Mean I Have to Shuffle My Boxcars?

You can't turn on the television without seeing at least one do-it-yourself program, ranging from building houses to remodeling to buying real estate! DIY knowledge is a very good thing; but in some areas, it's simply better to rely on an expert. Changing oil in your car is one thing, but making repairs to the transmission is quite another if you're not a skilled mechanic! The same thing applies to retirement planning. Making an outline and gathering information is very important; however, determining where your best investment opportunities are and how to diversify them is a financial advisor's job.

Because everyone is different, you may find the broad recommendations you hear on radio and television aren't a good fit. It's tough to determine how much money you'll realistically need in retirement, especially if you try to judge things on your own. It's important to have guidance from someone who not only is watching stocks and bonds and crunching numbers every day, but also to take advantage of the greater wealth of knowledge your financial planner has in all aspects of retirement.

So, let's get to the heart of the matter – you've thought about what you'd like to do in retirement, you've taken a look at your assets and expenditures. You've gathered all your financial information, checked out your retirement plans and reviewed the numbers. Now it's time to crunch and determine if you have enough for your retirement. What's enough? While it can be relative, enough is probably more than you expect! Remember, you want to maintain your living standard and replace your current income, and keep that money coming for what could be the next 30 or 40 years.

For our purposes, I'm recommending a beginning withdrawal rate of 5% to 7½% a year. That's the amount you'll transfer from your portfolio as your "retirement salary." That amount may increase as you age, depending upon the value of your portfolio and its returns, as well as your needs.

Just how often will you tap into your portfolio to get your "paycheck"? Some folks prefer to do it monthly while others recommend quarterly withdrawals.

Wage and Pension Worksheet

This is the Georgetown Capital Group Wage & Pension Worksheet. It's an effective and easy way to estimate how much money you'll need to "make up" after considering your pension and taxes. In other words, crunching these numbers en sures you'll be able to maintain your current standard of living well into retirement.

Our example here is Sarah, a married 53-year old utility company secretary. She grosses close to $40,000 annually and would like to retire at the end of this year. After checking out the Wage and Pension Worksheet, Sarah found she can retire, if she can make up a shortfall of about $7,300 a year.

Wage Income		You	Example
1. What is your *net* take home pay?		_____	$550
2. Credit union or bank deposits?	+	_____	+ 50
3. Net Disposable Income	=	_____	$600
4. Multiply by number of paychecks	x	_____	x52
5. Annual Disposable Income	=	_____	=$31,200
Pension Income			
1. Pension Income		_____	$ 2,500
2. Survivorship Option	-	_____	- 7%
3. Taxes	-	_____	- 15%
4. Net Pension	=	_____	=$ 1,989
5. Months per year	x	_____	x 12
6. Annual Net Pension	=	_____	$ 23,868
Shortfall To Make Up			
1. Annual Disposable Income		_____	$ 31,200
2. Net Annual Pension	-	_____	- 23,868
3. Cash Flow Shortfall	=	_____	$ 7,332

Now it's time for Sarah to decide where her $7,332 shortfall will come from – which accounts will she tap to make up the difference? Her best source of this retirement income is her IRA.

IRA Withdrawals

If, like Sarah, you're retiring prior to age 59½ and want to use money from your IRA, you may be worried about penalties. Believe it or not, there is a way for you to tap into your IRA, take out money before you're 59½ and not pay penalties! It's called IRS rule 72(t) and it benefits those who wish to leave the workforce before 59½.

Let's look at two examples, Sarah and Bob. As we mentioned, Sarah is 53 and plans to retire at the end of the year. While she will receive some pension income, she still needs to make up the shortfall of $7,332. Sarah can withdraw from her traditional IRA without penalty *if* she does some planning.

IRS rule 72(t) states that the 10% distribution penalty will be waived for distributions that are "part of a series of substantially equal payments of employee's life expectancy." Additionally, you need to take the income for at least five years and reach 59½. However, if you in any way alter your distribution amount from the original IRA, that pesky 10% penalty, plus interest, will be imposed on every dollar withdrawn since you started your IRA withdrawals!

So, Sarah wants to use her $125,000 IRA first before tapping other portfolio dollars. To do so, she must stick to her distribution schedule for 6½ years, until she's 59½. At that age, you can withdraw whatever amounts you need from retirement accounts without penalty.

If Sarah's IRA uses rule 72(t), and she uses a 7% distribution calculation, she'll be able to withdraw 7% of $125,000, or $8,750 per year, or $729.20 per month. The $8,750 annual distribution less 15% tax will generate $7,437 of after-tax income, which is equal to the shortfall difference between her current disposable income from her wages and the anticipated pension income after tax.

There is another catch to rule 72(t). It comes into play for Bob, who retires at age 57. His IRA contains $100,000 and he wants to set up a distribution schedule of equal payments. Will Bob be able to tap into his IRA for 2½ years and then withdraw more money without penalty? The answer is no – because Bob retires at age 57, he must stick to his distribution schedule for five years – the minimum amount of time you can withdraw from your IRA without penalty. So, after age 62, Bob can alter his IRA withdrawals.

Here's one more example. Fred is 59 and plans to retire next year, when he's 60. With his traditional IRA, Fred can withdraw from that account without penalty anytime after he's 59½. He even can allow the money to continue growing – but he must begin receiving the required minimum distribution from that IRA in 11 years, when he reaches 70½. In fact, he'll have to begin withdrawals by April 1 of the year after he turns 70½. The IRS determines how much you'll have to take out based upon life expectancy charts, and if you somehow don't take that minimum required distribution, the IRS will tax you 50% of the difference!

Once you are 70½, you don't need to take distributions from each IRA. You can calculate the required minimum distribution and take it from one IRA if you like or more than one IRA. If you have several IRA accounts, you may want to consider consolidating them. Your financial planner will be able to determine if there may be restrictions.

It's also important to note that in New York State the first $20,000 of income from your pension, IRA, 401(k) and annuity is exempt from state income tax each year after you are 59½.

Required minimum distributions are for IRA owners once they have turned the age of 70½ and have to be started by the April 1st after they're age 70½. As a example, if you turn 70 in March, you would be 70½ in September and you would be expected to take your required minimum distribution by December 31st of the year you turned 70½.

But by law, in the first year you have until April 1st after you're 70½, so in this particular case you can wait the following year April 1st, but also remember that in that year that you're 71, you would have to take out your second year's required minimum distribution, therefore forcing two years distributions into one. In most cases, everyone takes out their required minimum distribution in the year that they are 70½ and then every year thereafter.

Table for Determining Applicable Divisor

Age	Applicable divisor	Age	Applicable divisor
70	27.4	93	9.6
71	26.5	94	9.1
72	25.6	95	8.6
73	24.7	96	8.1
74	23.8	97	7.6
75	22.9	98	7.1
76	22.0	99	6.7
77	21.2	100	6.3
78	20.3	101	5.9
79	19.5	102	5.5
80	18.7	103	5.2
81	17.9	104	4.9
82	17.1	105	4.5
83	16.3	106	4.2
84	15.5	107	3.9
85	14.8	108	3.7
86	14.1	109	3.4
87	13.4	110	3.1
88	12.7	111	2.9
89	12.0	112	.2.6
90	11.4	113	2.4
91	10.8	114	2.1
92	10.2	115+	1.9

The calculations have gotten considerably easier recently, whereas (see the table attached) the individual turns 70½ and he or she has to take out 1/27.4 of their IRA value as of the preceding December 31st value. This has made the withdrawal divider much easier for IRA owners to comprehend and evaluate.

In many cases we come across IRA owners who have felt that once they turn 70½ they've got to withdraw all of their money out of their IRA, which would obviously force most people into an extraordinarily high tax bracket. If you had $100,000 in an IRA, you might think that you have to take out $100,000 out in the year that you are 70½ and be ratcheted right up to the 28% tax bracket or more. Again, this isn't the case, and as you approach your 70th birthday you will notice that the calculation is much more favorable than one would think. When it comes to beneficiaries of IRAs, the laws have changed dramatically.

The IRA Beneficiary rules up until 2001 were vague and difficult at best to comprehend. The new rules make it very easy for people who inherit an IRA or who are the beneficiaries of an IRA to simply add their name to the IRA and use their own life expectancy calculation in determining how much money they have to take out. If someone were to inherit an IRA and be hypothetically 40 years old and his or her life expectancy is another 50 years, he or she only has to take out about 1/50 or about 2% of the value of the account. The following year 1/49, then 1/48, then 1/47, etc., so the required minimum that a beneficiary has to take out is a small amount.

Beneficiaries can obviously take out as much as they want and even purge the IRA if they would like to, and obviously pay taxes on any income they take out in the calendar year that they take it out. But the law has made it very easy now for IRA beneficiaries to determine the mechanics that best suit them. In the case of multiple IRA beneficiaries, if parents pass away with, for example, four children, each child will get 25% of the parents' IRA. Each child will then have their own separate IRA worth a quarter of the value of the parents' account.

So under the current law, each beneficiary's IRA would be a stand-alone account and would not have any reference to a sibling or other beneficiarys as to how much or how little they would need to take out of their IRA.

In previous years, everyone had to take out a minimum percentage predicated on the oldest child or the oldest beneficiary listed on the account and it was at times a nightmare for any financial planner or IRA owner to figure out exactly what they had to take out or what they were entitled to.

Roth IRA

There are some benefits to having a Roth IRA when it comes time to take money out. First of all, Roth IRAs can be tapped without penalty and there's no minimum age requirement. However, the rules on withdrawals from a Roth IRA involve both profits and contributions.

If your Roth IRA is more than five years old, you can withdraw your profits tax-free if you meet these conditions: you're older than 59½, you're disabled, or you're a first-time homeowner (some specific rules apply here – it's best to talk to your financial planner before using this option). And after your death, your beneficiaries will not have to pay taxes on funds they withdraw.

A reason for the popularity of Roth IRAs centers on the flexibility to withdraw your initial contribution at any time, tax-free. But if you take out more, that amount is subject to income taxes if you don't meet any of the above requirements. And that pesky 10% penalty is there for folks under 59½.

Social Security Income

Another area where Sarah may be able to make up that $7,332 difference is through her Social Security Income. However, those dollars won't be added to the mix until she's at least 62.

Remember James and Kelly? In our example, they already have replaced pre-retirement income. In six years, James will be eligible to collect Social Security income. That becomes a cost of living increase for them. Three years later, Kelly's Social Security will kick in, adding to their income.

Age to Receive Full Social Security Benefits

Year of Birth	Full Retirement Age
1937 or earlier	65
1938	65 and 2 months
1939	65 and 4 months
1940	65 and 6 months
1941	65 and 8 months
1942	65 and 10 months
1943-1954	66
1955	66 and 2 months
1956	66 and 4 months
1957	66 and 6 months
1958	66 and 8 months
1959	66 and 10 months
1960 or later	67

It's important to remember that the above chart sets the timeline for when you can collect your full Social Security benefit. Many people don't realize that they can collect Social Security prior to the age of 65, 66 or 67.

However, collecting these benefits early (as early as age 62) versus "full retirement" (as early as 65) or "maximum benefits" (age 70) means the amount you receive will be reduced. For example, if you begin collecting Social Security benefits at age 62, expect to receive somewhere around 77% of the amount you'd receive if you waited until age 66. Your financial planner can provide specific details.

I generally advise clients to take Social Security as soon as they can, because none of us lives forever. There are programs to calculate break-even points to determine how long you need to live to see if it's worthwhile waiting for full benefits. Here's where family history and genealogy play a role.

If everyone in your family lives into their 90s, you may consider waiting until you reach the age of 65 to receive full Social Security benefits. But, if your health is not up to par, or those in your family have had shorter life spans, taking your benefits as soon as possible means more money for you now!

You can tell it's a tough call to determine just when to begin collecting Social Security. Deloitte & Touche calculates the break-even point on how long on average a person lives after receiving Social Security is 12 years. It's truly up to you whether you see yourself living beyond age 74, and holding on for full benefits. Again, my philosophy is go ahead and take your Social Security benefits early.

Jim retired in 2002, when he turned 62. It wasn't easy for him to decide whether or not he should begin his Social Security payments. Jim wanted to use the extra dollars, but he also was looking for that larger payment that would come in 2005, when he turns 65. His Social Security benefits at age 62 would be $1,000 a month. At 65, he would receive about $200 more, or $1,200 a month. While $2,400 a year sounds like a good deal, it takes some time to reach the break-even point. In our example, if Jim collects his benefits from age 62 to 72, he'll have collected $120,000. If he waits and collects from age 65 to 72, while his monthly check was higher, he'll only have collected $100,800. That extra $19,200 would have been of much more use, had Jim known he would only live to 72.

Another concern many people have about early retirement is whether or not it will cut into their Social Security benefits down the road. In fact, it's not much of a factor. If you leave your job at age 57 and end Social Security deductions from your paycheck, when you retire, you will receive somewhere between 0 and 5% less than if you stayed at your job through age 62. If you leave at a younger age, say 52, your benefits may be somewhere around 10% less than someone who worked until age 62.

Pensions – Traditional or Lump Sum?

There are as many pension plans out there as there are companies. Whether you can withdraw from your pension plan in monthly payments or in a lump sum varies from employer to employer. Many offer choices while still others make all the decisions for you. There is one constant, though – pension income is taxable. Your financial advisor can help assist you in finding ways to delay some of those taxes. Let's take a look at a couple of plans.

A traditional pension may cover you alone, or you and your spouse. If you opt for sole coverage, your monthly check will be greater, but payments end with your death. If you determine your spouse will need your pension payments after you die, you'll want to see if a two-life pension plan is an option. Some pensions offer the option of your spouse continuing to receive the same payment you got as a couple while other options include choosing a smaller amount.

In this example, Daniel's employer is offering an incentive of $500 per month until age 62 if he accepts this special early retirement package. There are a number of large firms that can be very creative to offer special incentive packages to entice employees to retire early.

Some packages include adding years of age and service to your calculation in case you may not have accumulated enough years. This adds a bonus or Social Security bridge which could turn out to be $X per month until 62.

Daniel's company is offering a $350,000 Lump Sum Pension with a $500 bonus until age 62, or a $2,000 per month Traditional Pension with the same $500 bonus until age 62. Daniel is 55 years old and has 30 years service with his company. Additionally, he and his wife Penny have $150,000 in a 401(k) plan.

Survivorship Pension Options

Most pensions offer the employee a set monthly income for as long as he or she lives. When he or she dies, the income stops.

There are a variety of survivorship options where a married couple will take a reduced monthly pension and when the retiree dies, the spouse receives a portion of income for the balance of his or her life.

In our example with Daniel and Penny, Daniel's firm offers a survivorship option where if Dan takes a 7% reduction in his pension and he dies, Penny will receive 50% of Daniel's reduced pension for the balance of her life.

Daniel and Penny have decided to go for a two-life pension option so they'll both be covered. Here's how their monthly income breaks down:

	Daniel (alive)	Penny (survivor option)
Amount received per month:	$2,000	$2,000
Survivorship Discount	- 7%	- 7%
Total	$1,860	$1,860
Bonus Until Age 62	+ 500	0
Survivorship Option		x 50%
Monthly Income	**$2,360**	**$ 930**

A couple of things to note in our example – the bonus income is paid only to the employee and not the spouse. Also, if the spouse pre-deceases the employee, the pension reverts to the full monthly amount.

Some pension plans will lower the monthly income to the retiree once he or she starts to receive Social Security. General Motors, for example, will lower the monthly pension once the retiree reaches 62 and starts collecting Social Security benefits.

The biggest benefit of this plan is that you have guaranteed income – you'll always receive a check, every month. However, that check will not get any larger as time goes on. There are no cost of living allowances in a traditional annuity.

Now, with a lump sum payment, Daniel and Penny's situation changes a bit. They can take the $350,000 payment and roll it over into an IRA. Daniel and Penny still receive a monthly income of $2,000 or more (using rule 72(t) from his IRA) and still have $500 monthly bonuses until age 62. Additionally, Daniel and Penny now have more control over their money. They can choose to give themselves a cost of living increase, can be conservative or aggressive in their investments, can distribute extra payments, and will be able to keep their assets in the family name. But, there's no guaranteed income with a lump sum payment. A wise financial advisor can assist you in coming out ahead with a lump sum payment.

Let's look at Daniel and Penny's situation once more, checking out a traditional pension payment versus a lump sum payment.

Income from Traditional Pension

Monthly Pension	$2,000.00
Survivor Option	- 7%
	$1,860.00
Bonus Until 62	+ 500.00
Total	$2,360.00
Tax	- 15%
Net Take Home	$2,006.00
Months	x 12
Annual Disposable Income	**$24,072.00**

Currently, Daniel and Penny's after-tax income is $31,200. Subtracting the pension after-tax income leaves an after-tax shortfall of $7,128.

Here's an example of how Daniel and Penny can make up that shortfall:

Move $150,000 from the 401(k) Savings Plan into an IRA and take $11,250 in distributions. After subtracting 15% for taxes, their after-tax IRA income is $9,562.50.

Retirement Income Make Up

After-tax Pension Income	$24,072
After-tax IRA Income	+ 9562
After-tax Retirement	$ 33,634
Current after-tax income	- 31,200
Additional Income	$ 2,434

In this example, Daniel's take home pay has been about $31,200 annually. By taking income from his pension, or lump sum rollovers, the $500 company incentive and a rule 72(t) distribution from his 401(k)/IRA, we now see Daniel having about $2,400 of additional income per year.

Of course, Daniel can get a part-time job to make up any shortfall from his pension income if he did not want to start to take distributions from his 401(k). The figures are different when Daniel and Penny decide to take a lump sum pension. They've decided to take the lump sum of $350,000 plus the $150,000 in the 401(k) and divide the amount into two IRAs. The $500,000 is split up this way: $400,000 to be used for cost of living income and $100,000 for future growth.

That $400,000 allows for a greater annual income:

Monthly Income	$2,700
Bonus Until 62	+ 500
Total	$3,200
Tax	- 15%
Monthly Take Home	$2,720
	x 12
Annual Disposable Income	***$32,640***

Daniel and Penny now actually have more income available in retirement than they are receiving now — $1,440 more!

And that $100,000 in a growth IRA will stay there until age 59½ or later to be used as a cost of living raise. The IRA has the potential to generate up to $12,000 of additional income in the future.

Also, when Daniel turns 62, monthly income will increase by about $600 per month. He'll receive $1,100 from Social Security but lose the $500 bonus he and Penny had been receiving as a company early retirement incentive.

A Quick Review

- Are you considering "do-it-yourself" investing?
- Is it in your best interest to consider using a financial advisor who works with stocks, bonds and pension plans every day? Are your pension, IRAs, etc. simplified enough for you to handle, or would professional advice be worthwhile?
- Have you considered that your retirement "salary" needs may be more than you expect? Can you be as conservative as possible in determining your needs?
- Have you considered how to base your retirement "salary" on your current cost of living?
- Did you know there are methods of withdrawing from IRAs that can save you from paying penalties?
- Have you considered the benefits of taking your Social Security benefits as soon as possible (if you have a healthy portfolio)?
- Do you know the pros and cons of taking a lump sum pension?

Chapter 4:

Your Risk Tolerance

Just How Fast Will This Train Go?

When I was in my 20s, riding in a sports car (sometimes at a high rate of speed) didn't seem like a big deal. In fact, it was a fun and challenging thing to do. Now that I'm a little older and wiser, I'm not opposed to riding a motorcycle, but riding at high speeds (especially without a helmet) doesn't seem quite so prudent.

It's the same with your portfolio – having the bulk of your investments in the stock market doesn't seem like a big deal when you're young and you don't need to be quite so concerned about short-term performance.

A Risk Tolerance Profile Questionnaire is the best way for you to communicate to your financial planner just how comfortable you are with various levels of "risk." By answering the following questions as truthfully as possible, then checking your score and determining your asset allocation strategy, you'll best be able to work with your advisor to have your portfolio work as hard as possible for you.

Your Time Horizon

1. When would you expect to begin withdrawing money from your investments?
      a. ___ Currently or within 1 year
      b. ___ 1-3 years
      c. ___ 4-6 years
      d. ___ 7-10 years
      e. ___ More than 10 years

2. Once you begin withdrawing money from your investments, for how many years will you continue to do so?
      a. ___ all at once
      b. ___ 1-3 years
      c. ___ 4-6 years
      d. ___ 7-10 years
      e. ___ 10 years to lifetime

Your Risk Tolerance

Please circle your answer to each question. This will help your financial advisor and you to determine your general investment goals and objectives.

3. **Which of the following portfolio mixes best reflects your investment comfort level?**
   a. Chance of short-term declines is **high** with an opportunity for portfolio growth to **significantly exceed** inflation.
   b. Chance of short-term declines is **moderate** with an opportunity for portfolio growth to **moderately exceed** inflation.
   c. Chance of short-term declines is **low** with an opportunity for portfolio growth to **slightly exceed** inflation.
   d. Chance of short-term declines is **very low** with an opportunity for portfolio growth to **just keep pace** with inflation.

4. **Do you agree or disagree with the following statement:** *"I am willing to lose larger sums of money in the short term if I can enjoy potentially higher returns in the long term."*
   a. Strongly Agree
   b. Agree
   c. Disagree
   d. Strongly Disagree

5. **Generally, investments with the highest potential for gains carry the greatest risk of loss. The table below displays four scenarios for best and worst outcomes of a $100,000 investment in four hypothetical portfolios over a five-year period. With which of the portfolios are you most comfortable?**

Possible Outcome for $100,000 invested for five years.

	Worst Case	Best Case
a. Portfolio 1	$ 90,000	$300,000
b. Portfolio 2	$ 95,000	$250,000
c. Portfolio 3	$100,000	$200,000
d. Portfolio 4	$110,000	$150,000

6. What is your investment priority?
   a. Increasing returns
   b. Primarily increasing returns while also reducing risk
   c. Primarily reducing risk while also increasing returns
   d. Reducing risk

7. The graph below shows quarterly returns of a hypothetical investment over time.

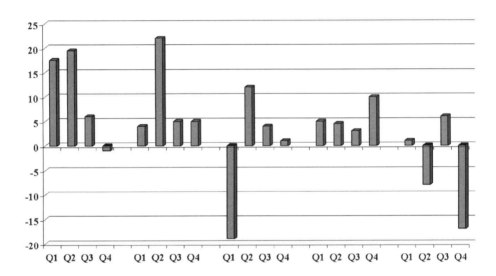

If you owned this investment (given historical and current returns) what action would you take?
   a. Sell all of the investment immediately and cut my losses
   b. Sell some of the investment to reduce exposure to further losses
   c. Continue to hold the investment with the expectation of higher returns

8. With which investments are you most comfortable?
   a. Highest potential long-term return with larger and more frequent interim losses.
   b. Moderate potential long-term return with modest and frequent interim losses.
   c. Lowest potential long-term return with smaller and less frequent interim losses.

9. The graph below provides "best and worst case" values for a $100,000 investment in three hypothetical portfolios over a *one-year* period. With which portfolio are you most comfortable?

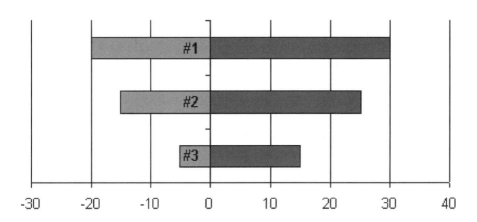

a. Portfolio #1 (downside of 20% - upside of 30%)
b. Portfolio #2 (downside of 15% - upside of 25%)
c. Portfolio #3 (downside of 5% - upside of 15%)

10. You've invested $100,000 in a portfolio that is expected to have high long-term returns and high short-term risks. The portfolio's value grows to $120,000 in the first year. If your portfolio lost all of its previous gains and some principal in the next month, how would you react?

a. I would not be concerned and would maintain the investment, knowing there continues to be potential for higher long-term returns.
b. I would be somewhat concerned and would shift into a slightly more conservative portfolio.
c. I would be very concerned and would shift into a much more conservative portfolio in an attempt to avoid further short-term losses.

11. **Which of the following investments has the characteristics you favor most?**
    a. Best chance of meeting long-term goals. Might have losses about one of every **three** years.
    b. Good chance of meeting long-term goals. Might have losses about one of every **four** years.
    c. Least chance of meeting long-term goals. Might have losses about one of every **ten** years.

Scoring Analysis

Use the following chart to interpret your scores. Circle the value that corresponds to each of your answers. Add up your score for each of the two sections and write down the total figure below. You'll need them for the next stage: Select Asset Allocation.

Time Horizon

	a	b	c	d	e
1	0	2	5	8	14
2	0	1	2	4	7

Risk Tolerance

	a	b	c	d
3	13	9	5	0
4	9	6	3	0
5	11	7	4	0
6	10	7	4	0
7	0	5	13	
8	10	5	0	
9	13	6	0	
10	10	50	0	
11	11	5	0	

Select Asset Allocation Strategy

Use your total scores from the questionnaire to determine which of the asset allocation models in the chart below best match your Time Horizon and Risk Tolerance. Find your Time Horizon scoring range on the vertical axis and the Risk Tolerance scoring range on the horizontal axis. Where the values intersect may be the appropriate asset allocation model for you.

For example, if your Time Horizon score was "9" and your Risk Tolerance score was "32" then your asset allocation model would be "Intermediate-Term/ Moderate.

Once you've determined your asset allocation model, refer to the following charts that reflect that model. This will be your individual asset allocation strategy for building your portfolio.

Please Note: Your advisor may use his or her own asset allocation models for your personal financial situation. Be sure to consult with your advisor before making any investment selections on your own.

RISK TOLERANCE

Time Horizon	Risk Factor		
	0-25	26-75	76-100
1-3	Short-Term Conservative	Short-Term Moderate	Short-Term Aggressive
4-5	Short-Term Conservative	Short-Term Moderate	Short-Term Aggressive
6-8	Intermediate-Term Conservative	Intermediate-Term Moderate	Intermediate-Term Moderate
9-10	Intermediate-Term Conservative	Intermediate-Term Moderate	Aggressive
11+	Long-Term Conservative	Long-Term Moderate	Aggressive

Phases of Investment Planning

Asset Allocation Model
Model: Short - Term Conservative
(Time Horizon 1 - 5 years)

Fixed Income	**90%**	**Domestic Equity**	**10%**
International Bond	5%	Large Cap Growth	10%
High-Yield Bond	10%		
Short & Int. Bond	35%		
Cash Equivalents	40%		

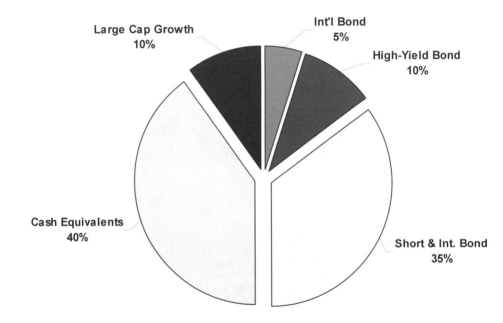

Asset Allocation Model
Model: Short - Term Moderate
(Time Horizon 1 - 5 years)

Domestic Equity	25%	Fixed Income	65%
Large Cap Growth	5%	High-Yield Bond	5%
Large Cap Value	10%	Short & Int. Bond	30%
Small Cap Equity	5%	Cash Equivalents	30%
Mid Cap Equity	5%		
		Int'l Equity	**10%**
		International Equity	10%

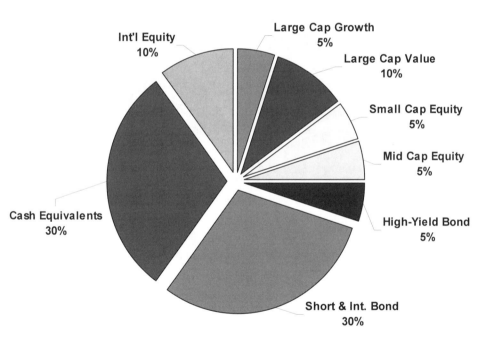

Asset Allocation Model
Model: Short - Term Aggressive
(Time Horizon 1 - 5 years)

Domestic Equity	**40%**	**Int'l Equity**	**15%**
Large Cap Growth	10%	International Equity	15%
Large Cap Value	15%		
Mid Cap Equity	5%	**Fixed Income**	**45%**
Small Cap Equity	5%	High-Yield Bond	5%
Real Assets	5%	Short & Int. Bond	20%
		Cash Equivalents	20%

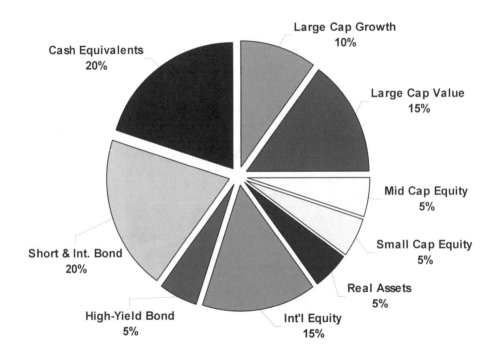

Asset Allocation Model
Model: Intermediate - Term   Conservative
(Time Horizon 6 - 10 years)

Domestic Equity	20%	Fixed Income	70%
Large Cap Growth	10%	International Bond	5%
Large Cap Value	10%	High-Yield Bond	10%
		Short & Int. Bond	35%
Int'l Equity	**10%**	Cash Equivalents	20%
International Equity	10%		

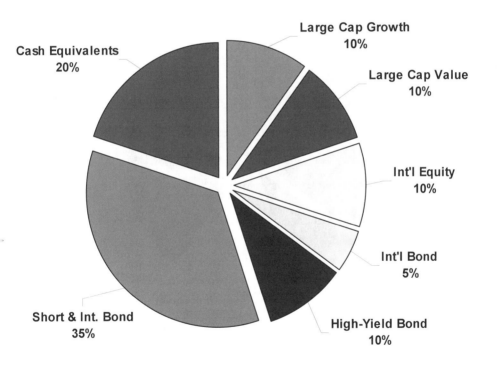

Asset Allocation Model
Model: Intermediate - Term Moderate
(Time Horizon 6 - 10 years)

Domestic Equity	45%	Fixed Income	45%
Large Cap Growth	20%	High-Yield Bond	10%
Large Cap Value	20%	Short & Int. Bond	25%
Mid Cap Equity	5%	Cash Equivalents	10%

Int'l Equity	10%
International Equity	10%

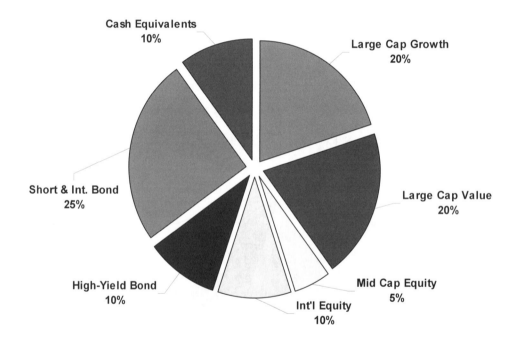

Asset Allocation Model
Model: Intermediate Term Aggressive
(Time Horizon 6-10 years)

Domestic Equity	**60%**	**Int'l Equity**	**15%**
Large Cap Growth	20%	International Equity	15%
Large Cap Value	20%		
Mid Cap Equity	10%	**Fixed Income**	**25%**
Small Cap Equity	10%	Short & Int. Bond	25%

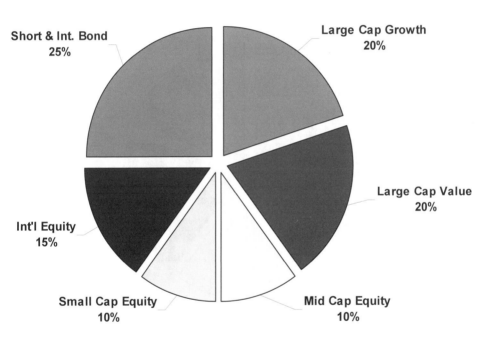

Asset Allocation Model
Model: Long - Term Conservative
(Time Horizon 10 - 15 years)

Domestic Equity	**50%**	**Int'l Equity**	**15%**
Large Cap Growth	20%	International Equity	15%
Large Cap Value	20%		
Mid Cap Equity	10%	**Fixed Income**	**35%**
		High-Yield Bond	10%
		Short & Int. Bond	25%

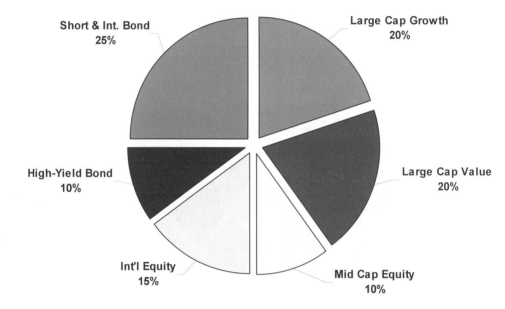

Asset Allocation Model
Model: Long - Term Moderate
(Time Horizon 10 - 15 years)

Domestic Equity	60%	Int'l Equity	15%
Large Cap Growth	25%	International Equity	15%
Large Cap Value	20%		
Mid Cap Equity	5%	**Fixed Income**	**25%**
Small Cap Equity	10%	Short & Int. Bond	15%
		High-Yield Bond	10%

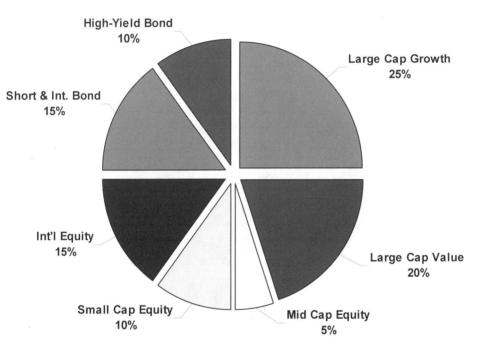

Asset Allocation Model
Model: Long - Term Aggressive
(Time Horizon 10 - 15 years)

Domestic Equity	85%	Int'l Equity	15%
Large Cap Growth	25%	International Equity	10%
Large Cap Value	20%	Emerging Mkts Equity	5%
Mid Cap Equity	10%		
Small Cap Equity	15%		
Specialty	15%		

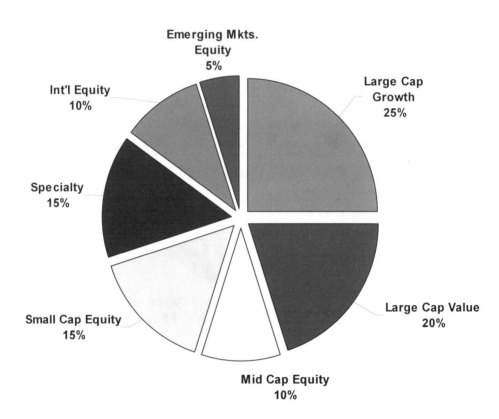

Empirical evidence shows that over 90% of the variation in returns experienced by a portfolio is a function of the portfolio's asset allocation.* In other words, choosing the right objective means establishing the percentage of investable assets to be allocated to equities, fixed income and cash. Within these broad asset classes, further diversification is required to optimize the risk/return relationship. Equity allocations may include large-cap domestic, mid- and small-cap domestic and foreign stocks. Fixed income allocations may include taxable and tax-free bonds.

* *Source: Brinson, Singer, and Beebower - Financial Journal*

A Quick Review

- What is your risk tolerance? Just how comfortable are you with higher levels of risk?
- Do you have a mix of funds, bonds and stocks, and other investments in your portfolio?
- Does your age play a role in your mix of stocks and other investments? Are you able to determine the best mix?
- Have you ever rebalanced a portfolio? Are you ready to put in as much time as necessary to learn all the ins and outs of doing so?

Chapter 5:

Rebalancing Your Portfolio

Preparing the Train for the Route

Let's get back to that game of "Operation." Remember how, if you didn't have the steadiest of hands, the game would buzz at you and let you know you made a mistake? If only rebalancing a portfolio was that easy! Unfortunately, there are no buzzers and bells to alert you of inadvisable moves or tax complications.

Because rebalancing is a delicate area, you may want to seek assistance from your advisor. Rebalancing helps make certain your investments are hard at work for you. It also improves your portfolio's performance. As I mentioned before, concentrating all your investments in just one company can spell disaster.

I can't say it enough – if you have an emotional attachment to a consistently underperforming stock, you're hurting your portfolio in the short and long term. While stock investments are long-term commitments, there are times selling is a sensible thing to do. Perhaps the stock is losing ground due to legal problems or management problems. Maybe the entire industry is lacking. Unless you're closely monitoring the stock market every hour of every day, you may not have the experience to know when to make a move and when to hold on to your stock.

As we discussed earlier, you'll want to decrease your stock percentage and increase your fixed income percentage as you grow older. Your financial advisor is there to help make changing this ratio as easy as possible.

Let's take a look now at some suggested phases of investment planning and determine a proposed mix of stocks and bonds for your portfolio, depending upon your age.

The following allocation models are being recommended in response to your risk tolerance profile. This is only a generic model and will need to be reviewed from time to time. The actual investment selection will be made by you and your financial consultant. Please note that your actual asset allocation may differ from this model due to special circumstances such as: other investments in 401k and pension accounts, inheritances, real estate, cash flow needs, etc.

Phases of Investment Planning
Age: Up to 40 Years
Balance: Up to 100% Stocks

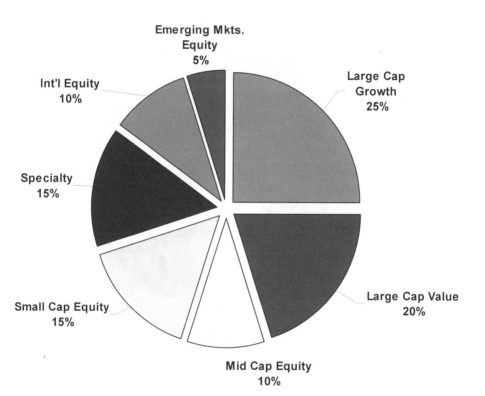

Emerging Mkts.
Equity
5%

Int'l Equity
10%

Large Cap
Growth
25%

Specialty
15%

Small Cap Equity
15%

Large Cap Value
20%

Mid Cap Equity
10%

Age: 40 to 50 Years
Balance: 75% Stocks & 25% Bonds

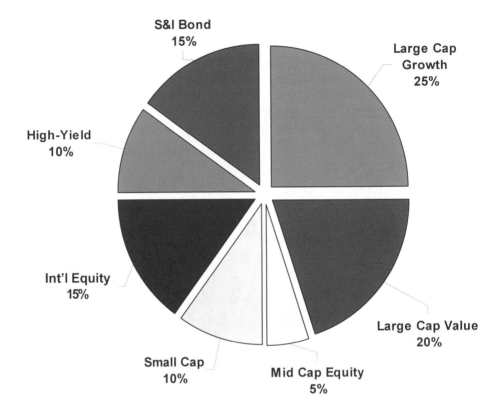

Age: 50 to 60 Years
Balance: 65% Stocks & 35% Bonds

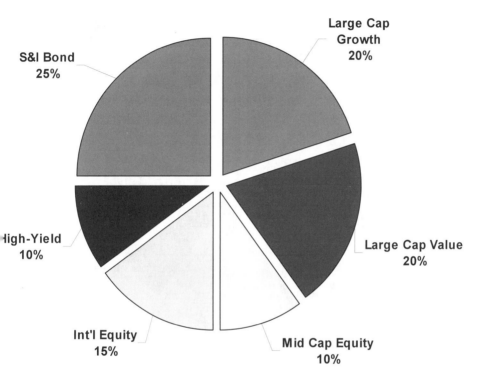

Large Cap
Growth
20%

S&I Bond
25%

Large Cap Value
20%

High-Yield
10%

Int'l Equity
15%

Mid Cap Equity
10%

Age: 60 Years Old & Retired
Balance: 55% Stocks & 45% Bonds

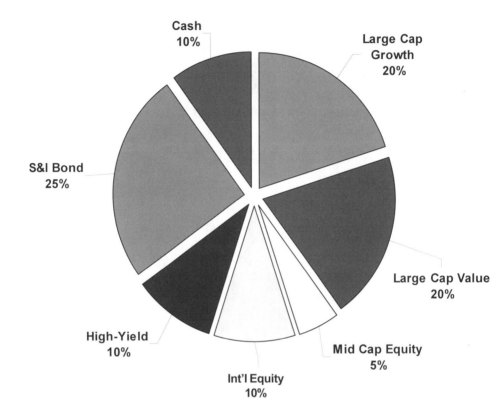

Generally speaking, in your 50s, you can have about a 60/40 mix in your portfolio. That's about 60 percent of your investment in the stock market and 40 percent in bonds. As you age, the mix changes. Around age 65, you may want to aim for a 50/50 split. And in your 70s, it's a judgment call, depending upon your preferences for your children's inheritances, etc.

This way, you're not basing your investment strategy solely on averages. You're pulling back as you age so that if there is another downturn in the stock market, you'll have time to recoup any losses. It's done by adding fixed income to your portfolio, providing stability.

So now, after taking a closer look at your risk tolerance, you and your financial advisor may decide it's best to do some rebalancing. On the face of it, it doesn't look too complicated – just shift some things here and move others there. However, it's very important to have professional advice when it comes to rebalancing. Government rules on IRA withdrawals and transfers along with tax implications make rebalancing a delicate process, similar to playing the board game "Operation" and removing the appendix. In the next chapter, we'll take a more in-depth look at rebalancing.

A Quick Review

- Are you investing with your heart and not your head? How are you choosing which mutual funds and stocks you hold?
- Have you had a big change in your life? Have you married? Are you divorced or have you experienced a long-term illness? Did you receive an inheritance? Rebalancing your portfolio is an important process and must be done whenever things change in your life.
- Are your investments age-appropriate? How much of your money is in stocks? How much in bonds? Do you know what percentage of your money remains in stock after your retirement?
- Is rebalancing something you're willing to do alone?

Joe Curatolo discussed the markets with ABC News commentator George Stephanopouls in Boston in 19

Joe and his wife Kathy swapped war stories with General Norman Schwarzkopf at a fundraiser in Buffalo in 1997.

NFL Hall of Famer Mike Ditka got some tips from Joe on how to "score" in investments in Boston in 1998.

Former President Gerald Ford was on hand in Palm Springs, California to honor Joe as one of only ten people enshrined into the Royal Alliance Associates Hall of Fame in 2001.

In 1996, Sir John Templeton provided some valuable insights into mutual funds to Joe and his wife Kathy at Templeton's headquarters in the Bahamas.

National and local media often seek Joe's insight into the market. Here he discusses retirement tips with Jodi Johnston of WGRZ-TV in Buffalo, NY.

The financial advisors and staff of Georgetown Capital Group

Chapter 6:

Investment Guidance

The Investment Train Engineer

There's the investment train – your cars include IRAs, pension funds, 401(k) accounts, savings accounts, stocks and bonds, and Social Security, to name a few. You've managed to get some good investments together, but just what kind of an engine do you have? Do you know how to operate it? In what direction should you go? How fast? While you may be able to navigate a bit, a skilled engineer knows the best routes, the safest methods, the most advantageous set-up of the cars, and optimum speed to get the train to its final destination. In other words, it's important to get help if you need it!

Seeking the Professionals

Investing is an area where most people seek professional help, and for good reason! Unless you're a qualified financial planner with many years devoted to learning this business, odds are there are gaps in your knowledge. You may have good intentions, planning to study and learn the best places to invest your all-important retirement funds, but never find the time. Or, you may consider your investment situation complicated enough that you don't want to get involved in the day-to-day management. Both situations end with the same result – hiring a professional.

Talking Heads

Whether it's on the radio or on television, there seems to be a quest for quick advice. You've probably heard or seen something like this happen: a qualified financial planner is discussing stock XYZ and its potential. He says things are looking good for this company and now is the time to invest! But is it the best time for *you* to invest? Should you run out and purchase stock in XYZ Company?

Let's examine this question further. Here's a possible scenario: This particular investment advisor only handles portfolios of $750,000 or more. He has determined that XYZ is a good investment for his clients, especially those who have the financial horsepower to invest $50,000 in this one area.

Or, perhaps this financial planner is a young hot shot. He's looking at XYZ Company's potential and growth as seen through his experience. When this planner was in kindergarten in the 1980s, XYZ Company had severe problems. However, because he's basing his "advice" on his experience and memory, this planner could be steering folks in the wrong direction.

Other things to consider — does the "talking head" have any ulterior motives in pushing the XYZ stock? How much money should *you* invest? How long would you keep funds in XYZ stock before selling? Is XYZ best bought with 401(k) funds? What makes it different from the ZYX Company, which is in the same business? Generally, these are questions that are not answered by the "experts" in their brief media appearances. And think of the audience! Is this advice just as valid for the 72-year-old retired plumber as it is for the 37-year-old engineer and father of two? Getting to know your financial advisor could be one of the best things you'll ever do for yourself, your family, and your retirement.

Peace of Mind

There's an awful lot to think about when it comes to retirement, and protecting your investments is just one piece of that pie. Are you prepared to spend at least several hours a month researching investments, determining where your dollars are best placed, monitoring performance of your stocks and bonds as well as other potential investments, and rebalancing your portfolio when necessary? It sounds like a full-time job, and it is! I devote at least eight hours a day, five days a week to stay abreast of everything happening in the financial world. To borrow an advertising phrase, "We live and breathe this stuff!"

Maintaining a large depth of investment knowledge is one reason Georgetown Capital Group clients have less anxiety about their retirement plan. Robert is a good example. An employee of a large communications corporation, Robert took early retirement at age 55 with a lump sum pension payment. Robert was concerned about meeting his day-to-day living costs because he had few other income-producing assets. He also was uncertain as to how to minimize taxes on that lump sum pension payment.

Robert called me looking for help. He told me he was not good at investing, didn't have the stomach for watching the stock market, and didn't have specific knowledge about retirement accounts. I set up a plan *specifically tailored to his needs*. It's still working well for him, and he's pleased with GCG and the service we continue to provide him. Robert is far less anxious when it comes to his retirement dollars and whether or not they're working best for him.

Your Input and Control

Your relationship with your financial advisor probably is similar to your relationship with your doctor. You need absolute trust in the person taking care of your health and the same goes for the person guiding your investment needs. Also, it's important you feel comfortable with your investment counselor and know he or she has your best interests at heart.

And just as in medicine, in financial planning, life experience counts. Financial planning involves some intensely personal issues including your salary, your family plans, and your marriage. I've found over the years people are most comfortable with someone who can empathize with their situation.

Investing and what Stimulates the Economy

Money, and the way that money transfers from one party to the other, stimulates the American economy as well as every economy throughout the entire modern world. It's called the velocity of money. The velocity of money is one of the most important characteristics of an economic system and how that system prospers.

The U.S. economy has three major factors, or engines, of spending where activity is created. They are in the business community, the consumer, and the government. You can think of it as a three-legged stool. You have to have at least two of the three economic engines working hard for our economy to prosper.

In the business community it is quite evident that in the mid to late 1990s, businesses were spending money hand over fist, and they spent it at an unbelievable pace. There was a tremendous amount of euphoria in the 1990s. The economy was fast-moving, unemployment was dropping, inflation stayed low, and equity investors were prospering. As we approached 1996 and 1997, there was a fear of Y2K, and that computers and the economic system that was run by electronic mechanisms might fail when we moved from the 1900s to the year 2000.

Through all of this fear, businesses spent money at an unprecedented pace to replace equipment, so they had to gear up for their systems to be Y2K compliant. In many areas, contracts could be broken and long-term agreements would be suspended if a party or a business venture was not Y2K compliant. Therefore, the software and computer industry was booming. The whole technology revolution was unbelievable, and the productivity of America was leaping in unprecedented paces as American industry spent unbelievable amounts of money to update their equipment to be compliant. In essence, they spent what some people say was five to seven years worth of technical expenditures in one to three years. Therefore, they ended up spending so much money that they borrowed from future spending years and brought it into current years. They consumed so much in inventory and upgrading that they robbed future years of spending. Computer companies of the world had three of four years of feast followed by what is now known as at least a few years of famine.

The massive engine of spending in the business community was phenomenal in the 1990s but came to a screeching halt in March of 2000. That leg of the three-legged stool of economic spending in essence vaporized itself, and that is the main reason why the U.S. economy went into a recession in 2001 and 2002.

One of the other three engines of the economy is consumer spending. Fortunately, consumers represent 60 percent of the economy when it comes to spending, and consumers have been spending right along. But if you think about it, that's what they generally do. Consumers get their paychecks whether it's weekly, bi-weekly or monthly and they spend it. They'll save some money, but they generally spend everything that they get when they get it. If someone is sitting on a 401(k) plan or has a systematic investment plan in place, they'll execute that savings rate, but everything else they generally spend.

While the economy was racing in the business boom of the 1990s, the consumer did not spend with that same euphoria, which is very fortunate. The wealth creation of the 1990s was more on paper than anything when it came to the consumer. The consumer did not spend lavishly and excessively as one would say the business community did. Consumer spending has been fairly consistent during the 1990s as well as during the recession of 2001-2002. Even though there have been two million American people out of work since the end of 2000, the rest of the consumers are spending quite nicely.

Interest rates have come down considerably since January 2001, which relates to lower mortgage rates and consumer interest for autos, home equity loans and general borrowing costs. Americans who do have jobs are not hesitant to buy cars or homes and to spend money on the normal activities that they generally do.

The third engine of spending is government spending. The government takes in huge sums of money through business taxes, consumer taxes, income taxes, tariffs, etc. and the government spends money. During the 1990s the government took in more than it spent and created a surplus of unspent money. In essence, the government was hoarding tax money. They were bringing it in but not spending it.

So when it comes to the velocity of money and the fact that money should be spent in the three areas that we've just discussed, businesses in the 1990s spent money ferociously. It was unbelievable the way that they spent money; it was feast and then famine.

Consumers, on the other hand, were much more stable, plodding along as they spent what they earned; and we didn't have the extreme peaks and valleys.

The government, being the third element, was spending but not as much as it was taking in. It was taking in more money, which is why it was creating these surpluses. When it comes to cash flow, the government was taking money out of the economy through taxes, but not putting it back in through military spending, road projects, civil projects, etc., where it helps municipalities, schools, or education grants. The government was taking in more money than it was putting out, so the government was siphoning off economic activity.

As the recession of 2001 is reviewed, we see only the consumer spending money. Business and government were not spending to the degree they should have. And with only one engine working, our economy has stalled.

Now the recession comes along. As an example of the current environment, businesses have been frozen for about two years of spending because they spent so much in the late 1990s. Consumers are chugging along, and now the government has to dramatically reduce interest rates to stimulate the economy. By lowering interest rates the government is basically telling the consumer and business people, *"Don't save money— go out and spend it"* which is how you get out of a recession.

By lowering Treasury bond rates from hypothetically 7% to 4%, it is telling the consumer, *"There is no great incentive for you to save money in bonds because we're not going to give you that great of an interest rate, so you may as well spend it."* If you look at money market interest rates, which in early 2001 were yielding approximately 6% and by early 2002 were approximately 1%, you see no real incentive in saving money or keeping it in a money market account. That's exactly what the government has been doing by lowering interest rates.

Their job is to create an incentive to spend. By lowering interest rates, people feel more comfortable in buying homes. As we know now, interest rates for mortgages dropped from about 8% in 2000 to 5½% in 2002. Therefore, homeowners can refinance and have stronger cash flow in their monthly budget, or possibly purchase a more expensive house with a lower mortgage interest rate so their overall mortgage payment will not go up dramatically.

Corporations and even municipalities can refinance in a manner similar to homeowners refinancing their loans. Therefore, corporations or municipalities, whether it's General Motors or the City of Miami, can go to the marketplace and refinance those existing bonds that may be paying 9%, and refinance them at 7% or even 4%. If you are a business owner there is an incentive for you to go out and build a factory, build a plant, hire people because you could borrow cheaper and it might be more economically feasible for you to expand your facility.

These are the three main areas of U.S. spending, and when you review what is going on in the economy as an investor or as a business person, these are the things that you should be looking at. With the government also creating a stimulus package by lowering tax rates slightly, they are trying to push money out of the system and into the economy. The one thing the government doesn't want to do is to flood the economy with too much stimulus that would create a knee-jerk reaction to the problems we have at hand. That would in effect force them to retract that stimulation later on; and the marketplace and the business community does not like whipsaw knee-jerk reactions. More of a gradual stimulation or a solid stimulation that might last for years is appreciated more than a stimulus package that is a quick shot in the arm, knowing that it will be over with shortly, and that the economic benefit will be short-lived.

A Quick Review

- Are you easily swayed by what you hear on radio or television? Are you willing to take general advice and apply it specifically to your situation?
- Are you disclosing all financial information to your advisor? Are you concerned he or she may be judgmental?
- Do you trust your financial advisor? Do you have a good relationship with him or her?
- Have you taken an interest in your portfolio? Are you asking your advisor about investment advice you've heard "on the street"?
- Do you feel confident your financial advisor has your best interest in mind?

Chapter 7:

Insurance

Having A Casey Jones On Your Side

The "what ifs" – you know, those crazy thoughts you have while you're on vacation: What if I left the oven on? What if I forgot to lock the garage door? What if the power goes out while we're gone? It's easy to keep going with "what if" thinking.

However, insurance is one useful way to reduce those "what if" concerns. I need to mention that by including insurance in this book, I'm expressing my opinions and not offering general or specific advice on insurance matters, nor am I offering or soliciting any insurance services.

That said, let's take a look at some types of insurance and examine the role insurance may play prior to and in your retirement. Insurance sometimes appears to be a luxury or a waste of money if you don't truly understand what it is you're getting from your policies. It is peace of mind, first and foremost, but insurance also can offer growth and protection of your assets.

Health Insurance

You may have heard the quote, "Perfect health, like perfect beauty, is a rare thing." A large part of all this planning for retirement is to enjoy it, live some dreams and do what you love. And while no one reaches retirement age in perfect health, insurance certainly plays a key role in helping us maintain good health. Without good health, retirement will not be nearly as enjoyable.

More importantly, without health insurance, the high cost of medical care could put a severe dent in your retirement portfolio. Check your pension plan benefits. Are you covered? Is your spouse? What type of plan is offered? Are you restricted to certain doctors or hospitals? Be certain your health insurance is renewable and non-cancelable.

Some companies offer you the opportunity to stay with their group health plan after you retire, quit, or are laid off. COBRA provides coverage for you for at least another 18 months, but you will have to pick up the cost charged to the employer, which can be high. As an alternative, you may be eligible for group health insurance through any organizations or groups you belong to – you'll want to check. Group insurance, on average, costs about 15% less than individual insurance.

There's also Medicare coverage, which is available to folks 65 and older who qualify for Social Security retirement benefits. I'll leave the details of Medicare to those more qualified to discuss it – but I will offer this information: if you are not getting Social Security, you should sign up for Medicare approaching your 65th birthday, even if you are not retiring. If you are receiving Social Security benefits, Medicare begins automatically at 65 years of age.

Disability Insurance

Thomas Edison said, "There is no substitute for hard work." As long as you are employed, disability insurance needs to be a part of the insurance puzzle, just as health insurance is. Disability insurance protects your income in case of illness or injury.

While disability insurance is similar to workers' compensation, there are differences. Workers' compensation replaces income due to injury, but only if that injury happens while you're on the job. Disability insurance kicks in regardless of where the injury occurs.

Some companies, mainly larger ones, offer disability insurance to employees. It may be a good idea to check to see if you have coverage, and if so, just what it covers. You may decide to apply for additional disability insurance on your own.

If you collect disability insurance and you paid the premiums, the money you receive is not taxed. But if your disability insurance is through your employer, you will owe taxes on the insurance money.

Once you're retired, you likely will not need disability insurance. However, it's a choice you should make after discussing the issue with a qualified insurance agent.

Long-Term Care Insurance

In Macbeth, Shakespeare wrote, "I bear a charmed life." Oh, if it were only so for the rest of us! No matter how much care or caution you take in your life, at some point a lengthy stay in a nursing home may be inevitable.

Family life has changed in our country. It's less common to see two or three generations under one roof, adult children caring for their elderly parents. Instead, we're mobile, we have dreams for our retirement that may not include living with our children, and we don't necessarily want to burden them with our care, should we need it.

Long-term insurance allows you to make preparations for your health care should you require some type of assisted living. Without long-term insurance, you may unnecessarily burden your spouse with health care costs, and you could spend much of the funds you've earmarked for your children's inheritances.

At today's prices, a good long-term care facility can cost anywhere from $45,000 to $100,000 annually! Pretty sobering to think about what that could do to your retirement portfolio.

But you can avoid that financial drain with long-term care insurance. This type of coverage typically covers some or all of the expenses associated with debilitating illness. To purchase long-term care, you need to be in reasonably good health. Plan specifics differ among insurance providers, so be certain to talk to your qualified insurance agent.

Here are a couple of examples of how some people are using long-term insurance:

Anne and Mark have been married for 26 years. Anne is 57 years old and Mark is 62 and retired. Anne worked part-time and stayed home with their two children, so both depend upon Mark's pension. They purchased long-term insurance about five years ago. Mark feels more secure about Anne's future should he suffer a stroke or other health problem because their nest egg of $500,000 would not be touched for his health care.

Mary is 57 and a widow. Her 25-year-old son just got married. She and her son are well off financially thanks to astute planning by Mary's husband. Mary wants to maintain that financial security, so she has purchased long-term insurance. Mary feels better knowing that if she suffers a serious illness the cost would be handled by insurance rather than by her son and his new wife.

Generally speaking, the cost of long-term care is reasonable. However, policy specifics can vary greatly, so be certain to do some comparison shopping.

Life Insurance

John Lennon and Paul McCartney wrote, "Ob-la-di, Ob-la-da, life goes on..." It may not be the most eloquent way of starting a discussion on life insurance, but it gives you a good idea of just what life insurance is for – those you leave behind. Life insurance is financial protection for your spouse and/or children if something happens to you. Life insurance also can help protect your estate from taxes.

Some people give up life insurance when they retire, or they are covered by small plans through their pension. Determining whether or not you should consider dropping life insurance protection is something best discussed with both your financial planner and your qualified insurance agent.

Generally speaking, if someone depends upon you financially, you need life insurance. But it's not that simple. Life insurance policies range from the simple to the extremely complex, making professional advice of utmost importance. Most people are familiar with two kinds of life insurance, term insurance and whole life insurance. Different insurance companies offer different variations of these types of policies.

Term insurance provides protection for a period of time (term). It's usually the least expensive insurance and has no cash value.

Whole Life Insurance builds up cash value and acts like a savings account. You can borrow against the policy.

To determine what kind of life insurance is best for you and your family, consult a qualified insurance agent.

Homeowners Insurance

"Be it ever so humble, there's no place like home." Your biggest investment is your home, and homeowners insurance protects your home, its contents, and provides some liability coverage in case you are sued. It's a good idea to review your policy every several years to make sure your coverage matches your possessions. If you've recently purchased computers, cameras, or jewelry, your coverage may not include these items.

If you have special items in your home such as antiques, artwork or rare collectables, you may want an additional rider on your policy. And what goes on outside your home may have an impact on the type of coverage needed as well. Floods and earthquakes require additional coverage.

Also, it's a good idea to ask your qualified insurance agent about discounts for items such as security alarms, smoke detectors, etc.

Auto Insurance

There's a popular sight gag in movies – I'm sure you've seen it. Somebody has parked a car on a San Francisco street. But the car doesn't stay parked for long. At some point, while the driver is standing near the car, talking to a friend, the car somehow starts rolling down the hill. Inevitably, someone asks, "Isn't that your car?" Then, hilarity ensues. In real life, such an accident would not be funny. And protection against accidents is just one part of auto insurance. Theft is another risk as well.

I know several people who drive Jeeps – according to police studies, their vehicles are 200% more likely to be stolen, on average, than just about any other car out there. That's a lot of stolen Jeeps! But car thieves and vandals aren't just targeting Jeeps. Many automobile owners across the country are victims of this crime.

Your automobile insurance policy ought to cover liability. You also need protection from insured and uninsured drivers. And, in the case of a driverless car rolling downhill, you'll need collision and comprehensive.

Again, it's a good idea to find out if your insurance policy offers discounts for automatic seat belts, air bags or alarms.

As you enter your retirement years, you may want to consider increasing your deductible on your automobile policy, as well as your homeowners insurance policy.

Umbrella Insurance

"Let a smile be your umbrella" may work for some people, but when it comes to insurance, you may need more than a smile for protection. This type of insurance gets its name straight from what it does – it sits on top of your homeowners and auto insurance, extending the liability of those policies.

An umbrella insurance policy could offer you extra protection in case of a multimillion dollar lawsuit for an automobile accident. Or, you might have someone fall while on your property, a child could be injured in your yard, etc. It's most important to read umbrella insurance policies carefully to make sure you have no gaps between your auto or homeowners policy and the umbrella policy.

Is umbrella insurance for you? If you answer yes to more than a couple of these questions, then it's a good bet you'll want to look into this type of coverage:

- *Do babysitters or cleaning people work in your home?*
- *Do you ever leave your home in the care of a house sitter?*
- *Do you have parties at your home?*
- *Do you have a swimming pool?*
- *Do you regularly drive children other than your own to events?*
- *Do you have a teenage driver?*
- *Are you involved in sports such as biking, skiing, boating or golf?*

If it looks like an umbrella insurance policy would be beneficial, the good news is that it's not expensive. Your qualified insurance agent can give you all the details.

A Quick Review

- When is the last time you took a good look at your insurance needs and determined the best coverage for you?
- Do you have enough health insurance? Do you know what insurance benefits are offered by your pension? Are you familiar with Medicare?
- Do you need disability insurance?
- Long-term health insurance is used more than any other kind of insurance. Have you explored taking out one of these policies? If you already have long-term insurance, have you added any insurance costs to your basic retirement "nut"?
- Is it a good idea for you to have life insurance after retiring?
- Do you have adequate homeowners insurance? Do you need an umbrella policy?

Chapter 8:

Stumbling Blocks and Mistakes to Avoid

Staying On The Best Rails

Five will get you ten we've all missed out on a great investment opportunity at some time. A friend of mine always tells the story of "the one that got away." She had the opportunity to travel to Seattle several years ago and met some people working with a computer software company. Over coffee, one thing led to another, and she learned that this company was planning to go public and sell stock.

When she returned to Western New York, my friend agonized over whether or not to buy stock in this company. She'd heard it could be a great deal, but decided in the long run she wasn't going to risk even $1,000 on this, and stuck that money in a CD.

I think you know the rest of the story. Every time a certain computer software company is in the news, my friend laments how "if only" she had taken that $1,000 and bought that stock, she could have parlayed it into thousands of dollars.

Inaction and Inertia

It's easy to remember the whoppers of mistakes – errors in judgment, allowing fear or greed to drive our financial decisions, only to result in losses. But as my friend's story illustrates, inertia, inaction, or not seeking professional advice is a common mistake that also can result in losses.

It's not even that complicated. One of the biggest errors I see today is employees not taking advantage of their employers' retirement plan programs. If your company offers a 401(k) plan with any sort of matching funds and you're not in the plan, drop this book and head on down to your human resources department now! Seriously, if you're not in a 401(k) plan, it is important to find out how and when you can get in, and do it.

Another area where we tend to remain complacent is credit card spending. It's easy to rack up hundreds of dollars in credit card bills, and pay only the monthly minimum. In today's market, you're likely paying at least 10% interest on those cards, with a high end of more than 21%. By not taking action and making a decisive plan to whittle down that debt, you're costing yourself a large amount of interest. That's money that could be going toward your retirement instead of lining the wallets of credit card companies.

It Looked Good At The Time...

Treasury bills, certificate of deposits (CDs) and money market funds all play very useful roles in investing for retirement. However, putting all or too much of your money in these areas can be damaging. Many people want to be conservative and keep their money safe, but inflation can do more damage over several years than an underperforming stock.

Let's look at two different retired couples – Martin and Anne, and Ted and Christine. These couples retired in 1985, at age 65.

Each couple had saved $300,000 for retirement. For Martin and Anne, all their retirement funds are in CDs. When they first began investing in CDs, the interest rate yielded about 8%. Ted and Christine sought professional advice for their retirement portfolio. Their financial advisor created a diversified portfolio.

As inflation declined, Martin and Anne continued to roll over their CDs. The rate of interest on those CDs declined sharply. About ten years ago, with a 4.5% return on their CDs, they had to dip into their principal to fund their retirement. Ted and Christine didn't have to touch their portfolio. With professional advice and a broad balance of investments, their principal grew enough for them to keep the principal intact.

Now, more than fifteen years after retirement, Martin and Anne have seen their portfolio decline to under $150,000, and they have a very real concern as to a complete depletion of their money. Ted and Christine are much better off. They've seen their principal more than double *and* have been able to withdraw money for trips, gifts, and other optional expenses.

The moral of the story here is simple – conservative investing can be a good thing, but you can have too much of a good thing. I can't emphasize enough the importance of getting professional advice to grow your portfolio for your retirement.

U.S. Savings Bonds

Savings bonds are another way to put aside some money for retirement. But here's another big blunder – holding on to bonds after they've stopped paying interest.

Series E bonds issued before December 1965 earn interest for forty years. Those issued after November 1965 stopped earning interest in 1995. Interest on these bonds can be deferred until you cash them in, so many people plan to cash them in retirement, while in a lower tax bracket. But if you own a Series E bond that was issued in January 1966, that bond has *earned no interest* for five years! That's money that just stopped working for you.

Series EE bonds earn interest for thirty years from the issue date. These bonds first were issued in 1980 and reach face value when they achieve what is called "original maturity." The bonds then continue to earn interest for thirty years from the issue date, but at various rates. Series I bonds are new. These bonds are "inflation protected" and are linked to the consumer price index and also earn interest for up to thirty years from the issue date.

Generally, it's difficult to calculate how much interest is owed on bonds, so going to the bank to cash them in can be dangerous. Your investment advisor can offer you the best advice when it comes to determining when to cash in your U.S. Savings Bonds.

Lack of Diversification

Some folks consider themselves very conservative when it comes to investing. Their risk tolerance profile results are very low. Often, we see these low-risk people limiting investments to money market funds, CDs and fixed-income securities, perhaps with some utility stocks thrown in. While that may seem to be diversification because not all the eggs are in one basket, all these investments are interest-sensitive. In other words, when interest rates go up, the value of their stocks and fixed-income securities will drop.

Another example of a lack of diversification involves over investing in your employer's stock. We discussed this earlier in the book, and it's one of the most common portfolio mistakes I see. Company loyalty is admirable, and many companies have done well over the years for their employees. But there's always the specter of "tomorrow" on the horizon. Enron Corporation employees, just eighteen months ago, were "all set" with their Enron stock-laden portfolios. What a difference a day made! With diversification, if one stock out of many underperforms, the other stocks can offset any losses.

Using Your Heart Over Your Brain

Trudy loved her grandfather very much. He was the one who got her interested in learning more about the stock market. Together, they'd read the newspaper, pick out stocks and do some "fantasy investing." When Trudy was sixteen, her grandfather gave her $500 to do some real investing in one of their favorite stock picks.

Over the years, Trudy's stock grew and performed admirably. At one time, Trudy had about $5,000 in this stock. A larger company purchased the little company and over time, Trudy's investment became static. Years later, her stock now is worth about $2,500 and in all likelihood will not go much higher. The reasons are varied – this particular company has done just about all the growing it can, its CEO is not taking any risks, and this particular sector has been down for quite a while. Even with all that in mind, Trudy continues to steadfastly hold on to "her grandfather's stock." That's her heart talking, not her brain.

Trudy's financial advisor offers her a much less emotion-laden opinion when it omes to this stock. It's time to sell and use the money in an investment that will vork harder for her. It was a tough sell to get Trudy to part with the stock, but now, everal years later, she's happy with the decision. That stock has dropped even ower and her $2,500 in a new investment already has doubled. Seeking professional advice, Trudy says, was one of the best things she ever did.

Another example of emotions over logic involves what some people call "the hangers-on." Harry is a "hanger." He bought a stock for approximately $3,000 everal years ago. Now, the stock's value hovers around $1,300 and has for the ast six years. But Harry won't sell. He's waiting for it to rise to his initial investment before he sells that stock. Once Harry met with his financial advisor, he recognized hat he's losing money on top of his initial losses by hanging on. Selling the stock, investing in a better performing stock, and cutting his losses has netted Harry more ollars than if that money had remained in his underperforming stock.

Balance, Balance, Balance

One of the most important things a financial planner offers clients is constant nonitoring of your portfolio. Often, a do-it-yourself investor can set up a fair mix of tocks and money market funds, but without careful monitoring and a professional's nowledge of the markets, things can go astray.

Here's a brief example: you began contributing $500 a month to your retirement account in 1985, investing half in Company A's growth mutual fund, the other alf in Company A's mutual bond fund. If you never rebalanced, your allocation oday would be 73% in the growth mutual fund and 27% in bonds. That translates o a riskier portfolio.

Also, beware of hidden problems. For example, Fred works for a great company. He has a 401(k) with a company match, stock options and an employee tock purchase plan. So, Fred has invested most of his 401(k) money in Company A's mutual funds rather than his employer's stock. Sounds like a good diversification plan, right? It's not. The second largest holding in Company A's mutual fund is – Fred's employer. Fred's financial advisor is outlining some long-term changes or Fred's portfolio.

A Quick Review

- Do you know an investment opportunity when it comes down the road?
- Are you too conservative in your portfolio?
- Do you hold on to poor investments for emotional reasons?
- Have you done your homework when it comes to making certain your port folio is diversified enough?
- Are you making certain all your assets are working for you? Do you hav old Savings Bonds that are not paying interest?

Chapter 9:

Taxes – What's Out There?

How Much of the Fare Must I Share?

While we all are willing to pay our fair share of taxes, today there are fewe and fewer ways to reduce the tax bill. In the last twenty years, major changes were made to the tax code, evaporating the vast majority of write-offs and deductions fo individuals and businesses.

Today, there are 90% fewer deductions than in 1980. And even though the maximum federal tax bracket in 1980 was 50%, with deductions your margina bracket may have been reduced to 20%. Today, while the highest tax bracket i 38%, due to fewer deductions, your marginal bracket only is reduced to 30%. Al told, we're paying more in income taxes today than we did 20 years ago.

Making the Most of Deductions

Because we have fewer and fewer ways of reducing our tax burden, the ques tion naturally arises, "How can I lower my tax bill?" Honestly, there aren't many things you can do today to create deductions. There just aren't a lot of deduction for wage income, which is your W-2 income from work. If you are self-employed and have 1099 income, you may have some specific deductions available. In gen eral, those deductions may be automobile use, expense, travel, entertainment, in ventory of goods, and some depreciation allowances, possibly including a hom office deduction (if it really is used as a home office). However, many previously allowed tax deductions no longer are permissible under IRS code and it's best t discuss things with your accountant.

If your income comes straight from your employer via your paycheck, you ca defer some taxes by investing in 401(k) or payroll deduction-type accounts, which we discussed in an earlier chapter. Or, depending upon your income level, you ma qualify to place $3,000 in an IRA for you and possibly your spouse. As we'v covered, placing funds in an IRA reduces your taxable income for that calenda year.

Other deductions include property taxes and interest on a mortgage or hom equity loan, but if your income is above a certain limit, those deductions are phase out. So, once again, the IRS has removed at least a portion of the deductions tha were common and available to everyone.

Complications

As if things weren't complicated enough, there are different tax rates for different types of income. Your investments are taxed at what's known as the capital gain rate. This rate applies for assets such as real estate or other investments owned for more than a year. The capital gain rate is a much more favorable rate than taxes on wages. For example, ordinary income from wages may be taxed as high as 38%, but the tax rate for an investment held for more than a year before being sold may be around 20%.

There's been some lively debate over the past ten years regarding elimination of capital gains, but all it is right now is talk. Some hope wiping out the tax would be an incentive for Americans to increase their investments in real estate, the stock market and other long-term investments. Hopefully, within the next three to five years, capital gains will be eliminated. I believe elimination of capital gains will free up a tremendous amount of capital – there are many folks holding on to assets to avoid tax ramifications who are petrified to sell.

It's likely most of the investors hoping to sell who instead are hanging on to their assets probably have their dollars in several areas, including real estate or mutual funds. The longer this money sits still, the more it affects the economy. Therefore, the great debate revolving around eliminating capital gains is backed by the anticipation of a much stronger economy in the U.S.

But those against elimination of the capital gains tax have some motive, and that motive is money. They continue the battle because they want the money generated for the federal government from capital gains. It sounds a bit like the chicken and the egg — does the government eliminate the capital gains tax and give up income that it currently receives; or does it eliminate capital gains and stimulate the economy by allowing individuals to more freely transact business to sell and buy long-term assets?

Mutual Funds and Capital Gains

One of the more difficult aspects of taxes on mutual funds involves annual capital gains distributions. Whether or not a mutual fund has a positive return for a calendar year has no impact on whether or not the mutual fund shareholder will have to pay taxes on the capital gains generated within the mutual fund.

Mutual funds, by charter and by-laws, have to pass on any realized capital gains to shareholders shortly after the fiscal year ends, generally in October. At the end of the year, the fund pays these gains to shareholders as income dividends or capital gains.

You can have capital gains even if the mutual fund had a negative return in one year. The formula to calculate capital gains takes the selling price and subtracts the purchase price. It doesn't matter if the fund's holding did not do well in one year if there was an overall gain – that means taxes.

Let's say in 1998, your fund purchased a security for $15 a share. At the beginning of 2002, the security is worth $30 a share. When the fund sells the security in mid-2002, its value is $25 a share. That's a loss for the year, but an overall profit of $10 a share. It can get even more complicated – if the fund sells the security for $35 a share, that's a capital gain. But if the rest of your fund's holding went south, resulting in a losing year, you still have to pay capital gains taxes on the security that was sold at a profit.

Remember our earlier discussions about IRA distributions for folks younger than 59½ and those older than 70½? It's important to remember that income from IRAs or a tax-deferred plan is taxed at a higher rate than capital gains rates. Funds received from an IRA are considered ordinary income, just like your salary, so taxes are higher than capital gains, which allows for a much more favorable income tax calculation.

Other taxes

As you probably have noticed when you look at your paycheck stub, your income also had additional taxes attached, including FICA and Social Security.

It's very important to keep up on those and other taxes. Tax rules are changing almost constantly, making things more difficult to understand. Every investor must keep up with how the new tax laws affect how much you owe the federal government. You also must have a strong relationship with a professional accountant. You need someone who has more than a pencil and a pad – you need a professional who knows current tax codes and will not hesitate to make suggestions to save you from future tax liabilities.

1 Quick Review

- There are 90% fewer tax deductions than there were twenty years ago. Even though the tax rate is lower today, your net tax rate is higher.
- Self-employed workers may have more deductions available to them than those who work for a business.
- Remember IRAs and 401(k) plans can help reduce your income taxes.
- Capital gains are taxed at a lower rate than income. There's much debate over capital gains and Congress continues to discuss the possibility of eliminating the tax, but it doesn't look like that will happen anytime soon.
- Capital gains from mutual funds are complicated. It's best to have a professional accountant to help you through the tax maze.
- Do you know an investment opportunity when it comes down the road?

Chapter 10:

Estate Planning and Gifting

Adding Specialty Cars to Your Train

Talking about estate planning is about as much fun as going to the dentist. It's necessary, but not enjoyable. However, estate planning is a very important topic. It s a means by which you can provide a substantial sum to help your children or other oved ones after you and your spouse are gone.

Death is not a popular subject. Here's a better way to look at this – estate planning is like giving your loved ones a wonderful gift. Careful planning allows you o make sure a big chunk of your estate does not get eaten up by legal expenses and axes. If you do not leave instructions in proper legal form, your assets will be lisposed according to state law, which likely is not the way you would choose.

And estate planning is about more than taxes – it's about what happens if you or your spouse becomes disabled, it's about the flow of taxes, and it's about your children's futures. Estate planning is definitely a place to get help from a professional.

Getting Help

Estate planning includes trust planning, writing wills, and dealing with laws and axes. Because it involves two rather complicated areas, it's important that these egal documents be done to exact specifications. State laws change frequently when t comes to estate planning. And estate tax code is lengthy and the fine print goes on and on. Please don't let this put you off – there are lots of excuses, including not understanding the terminology, finding the process intimidating, and just plain not wanting to think about death. An astonishing 50% of people die without estate plans. If you don't think about it now, your loved ones may get tangled up in a legal and financial nightmare.

I'll reiterate — it's important for you to take care of estate planning as soon as possible. If you're fifty or older and you don't have an estate plan, it's vital you get one as soon as possible. It truly is the best gift for your family.

Where to Begin

First, make an appointment to see an estate planner, and then keep that appointment! Next, gather some information. Start by reviewing your net worth statement and determine which assets you hold jointly and which are held individually. Also, prepare a schedule of life insurance policies. List the owner, the beneficiary, and the face amount. Retirement plan accounts and IRAs need to be considered as well, and be certain to know the death beneficiary designations. You'll also want to list any debts and if you owe a balance on your mortgage. Armed with this information, your trip to the estate planner will be less painful than the dentist.

Still, couples often wait on preparing an estate plan, thinking they can delay this step. Sometimes it causes a major problem that's a "time bomb." The problem arises not with the death of, say, the husband, but instead when his widow passes away.

When Jack passed away, he had $500,000 in his name and $250,000 in joint accounts with his wife Lydia. A marital deduction allows those assets to transfer to Lydia with no estate consequences. As the years go on, the portfolio grows to more than $1.5 million. Upon Lydia's death, only $1 million can be passed to her heirs free of taxes. The additional money is taxed at a very high rate – more than 40%— and Lydia's children are responsible for those taxes!

Most of those taxes could have been avoided if Lydia had seen an estate planner and created a special type of trust when Jack died. Much of the money could have gone into the trust for Lydia's use and the trust money (and its interest) will never be taxed again. There's more about trusts later in this chapter.

Leaving a Will

Preparing a will is a basic step in estate planning. Sometimes, all you may need is a simple will. Your will, essentially, is a legally binding document that determines how all your property will be distributed at your death. Property can be defined as just about anything, including your pets, valuables and any other possessions.

In your will, you can specify how debts, taxes, fees, and other costs are paid. Changes can be made to your will at any time up until death. Ideally, without big changes in your life, you should review your will once a year to determine if any changes need to be made.

Some of those changes may include marriage, divorce, death of a spouse, the birth or adoption of children or grandchildren, a move to another state or the death of a beneficiary. Also you'll want to consider any big financial changes, including leaving a job, inheriting money, or selling something with substantial value.

When a person dies, his or her will is probated. Joint assets are not included. During the probate process, your executor notifies your beneficiaries, and your will becomes a matter of public record. Your executor works with the court to review your assets and determine if any outstanding debts need to be paid. It also is the time estate and other taxes are paid, and final income tax returns are filed. After these steps are completed, your wishes are made known for disposal of your assets to your beneficiaries. Then, your estate is closed.

The biggest advantage to having a will is that any disputes about the disposition of your estate will be settled impartially through a probate court. But the costs of probate court are high, and it can take a very long time to resolve a dispute. The fees for the court are paid from your estate, so the longer it takes to resolve, more of your money goes to the court and not to your beneficiaries. And your will and all documents associated with probate become public record.

Another problem with probate is that if you own land in another state (not your legal residence), a separate probate is required.

Leaving a Trust

A trust often is the best choice for many people. It's a legal agreement listing specific assets in trust for any number of people you name. Those assets can include bank accounts, investments, real estate and personal property. Trusts traditionally allow flexibility, more control and tax benefits. Also, with a trust, you usually can avoid probate. You can set up a trust as a stand-alone document, or it can be part of your will.

There are two kinds of trusts: irrevocable and revocable. An irrevocable trust is permanent; it can never be changed. It is established when you are certain you are not going to change your mind about the transfer of any named assets. In other words, an irrevocable trust means you have renounced ownership of the assets you place in that trust. When an irrevocable trust is properly drawn it should not be subject to estate tax, but if you retain some rights to income from the trust, that income may be taxed when you die.

Some examples of an irrevocable trust are: an education fund for children or grandchildren, a fund for a charity, or monies to be used to help a family member who is permanently disabled.

A revocable trust is more like a will in that you can make changes at any time while you're alive. Because you keep the assets in your control, revocable trusts are more popular than irrevocable trusts. Those same situations listed above can also benefit from revocable trusts.

In general, revocable trusts are best used for estate planning because of their flexibility and ability to allow you to continue to manage assets in the trust. The terms of these trusts provide many choices, which allow you to make the most of the assets contained in the trust. Your financial advisor can help determine what kind of trust may be right for you.

Bequests

Most families determine that upon the death of the surviving parent, the balance of the estate will be shared equally among their children. While you certainly want to be fair, sometimes it's better to consider need rather than equality.

Dan and Donna have three children. After speaking with their Georgetown Capital financial advisor, they have decided not to divide their estate equally among their kids. Dan and Donna are sensitive as to how this might play out when the will is read, so they're stating up front that the children were loved equally, but their needs are unequal and provisions were made accordingly.

Some concerns that may lead you to determine if need is a concern: are any of your children active in a family business? Does one show more managerial potential than another? Is one child a minor? These questions would dictate whether or not a fair division of assets is the best solution.

Be sure not to punish a child because they are successful. Some parents don't give money to a child who has become financially secure, so that child may feel penalized for being prosperous.

Death and Taxes

These things may be inevitable, but tax laws seem to change almost daily. It's best to seek professional advice before setting up any wills or trusts. While those costs may seem high at the time, there could be greater costs down the road if estate plans are not set up properly.

For example, Alan and Lori thought that the fees for estate planning sounded a bit high, so they purchased a couple of books and some estate planning software to try to do it alone. The documents they use are just about word for word from the books and computer program, and look just as good as documents from any law firm. They have the documents signed, witnessed, and notarized.

But several years down the road, after Alan's death, his family finds out that while some of the estate planning holds up, another portion of it was not prepared properly according to laws in their state. Lori will survive financially, but after her death taxes on their assets will reduce their children's inheritance significantly.

Gifting

Estate planning doesn't necessarily lead only to dividing up your assets when you die. Often, it's in your best interest as well as your loved ones to find ways to give money to them while you are alive. There are tax benefits as well as the knowledge that you're helping your family members achieve greater goals.

Chuck and Melissa have been retired for more than ten years and through smart investment and retirement planning, their portfolio contains $1.3 million dollars. They have two married children and three grandchildren. Gifting allows Chuck and Melissa to give up to $11,000 to as many people as they want, helping to reduce the tax bite on their estate. So, Chuck can remove up to $55,000 per year from his estate in gifts to his children and grandchildren. The same goes for Melissa. So for the next four years they give $110,000 a year to their family members, allowing them to remove $440,000 from their combined estates. If Chuck dies first, all the money gifted to the family is eliminated from Melissa's estate, resulting in substantial tax savings.

For children under age fourteen, unearned income beyond $1,500 will be taxed at your marginal rate, so the benefit of gifting income to them is limited. But for children fourteen and older, their income (earned and unearned) will be taxed at their own marginal rates.

College Planning

Earlier I discussed several methods of saving money for your children or grandchildren's education. One included the EIRA (Educational Individual Retirement Account). Here's a look at a couple more ways to prepare for college costs while reaping some tax benefits.

529 Education Plan

Many families find this plan more appealing than an EIRA. The plan is known as a 529 Education Plan, named after Section 529 of the Internal Revenue Code. It has two main benefits: investments are allowed to grow free of federal income tax (however, you must pay state taxes); and it offers special gift tax exclusion. You can contribute up to $55,000 for each beneficiary every five years without federal gift tax consequences. Married couples can contribute $110,000 annually. But, you must not give any other "gifts" to the beneficiary for five years.

Parents and grandparents may rollover EIRAs into 529s. Funds from a 529 plan can only pay for college costs, including tuition, fees, room and board and other supplies, including computers. The IRS charges a 10 percent penalty if you use a withdrawal for non-qualified expenses.

529 funds also offer more flexibility than EIRAs. The money can pay for qualified expenses at any post-high school institution, including most vocational-technical schools. There are also no income limits on who can contribute to the account and no age restrictions on the beneficiaries.

Contributions to the account can continue until the total value of the 529 plan is

$246,000. After that, earnings can continue to grow, but no more contributions may be made. Beneficiaries don't have to be family members and you can even create a 529 plan for yourself. And, the beneficiary of the account may be changed to another family member at any time.

Some important points to remember:

- You can contribute $55,000 per beneficiary in the first year of a five-year period to avoid federal gift tax consequences ($110,000 per married couple).
- Effective January 1, 2002, earnings on 529 plans withdrawn for qualified expenses (tuition, room, board, supplies and fees) are not subject to federal income tax. Prior to this date, earnings will be taxed at beneficiary's tax rate.
- State tax exemptions or deductions vary by state of residence of the account holder. The most current information can be found at **www.savingforcollege.com** and **www.collegesavings.org**.
- You will control how the money is distributed, so you know it will go toward education expenses.
- If your child chooses not to go to college, or does not use all the assets in the account, you can change the beneficiary tax- and penalty-free as long as he or she is a member of your family and uses the money on qualified education expenses. (Qualifying members of family include father, mother, son, daughter, brother, sister, stepfather, stepmother, stepchildren, in-laws, spouse and first cousins of designated beneficiary).
- Non-qualified withdrawals are subject to income tax and a 10% penalty.

Stretch IRA

If you designated your children as beneficiaries of a traditional IRA, there's a minimum time frame in which they must liquidate the account after your death. Now the IRS has changed some rules to allow beneficiaries to inherit the money, tax deferred. That means the IRA can continue to grow and does not have to be cashed out in five years.

This Stretch IRA allows your beneficiaries to withdraw a minimum of 2% to 5% each year, based upon his or her age, with no maximum limit. There's also no probate on these accounts.

What this means when you're planning your estate is that you really have the opportunity to pass money onto your heirs instead of the taxman.

Tim was the beneficiary of his father's IRA. When his father died three years ago, the IRA was re-registered in both Tim's name and his father's name. So instead of being forced to liquidate the entire account within five years, under the new rules Tim can withdraw smaller amounts for home improvements and personal expenses.

The Stretch IRA helps to avoid large, lump sum taxable distributions and allows your beneficiaries to assume the IRA in their names. They then can name their own beneficiaries for the account. And if you name more than one beneficiary, these new rules allow the funds to be divided into separate IRAs for each beneficiary.

The only way to create a Stretch IRA is to register the specific beneficiaries of the account with the custodians of the IRA (most commonly a mutual fund). Tim has done so, and named his cousin as beneficiary, so his father's money continues to provide tax-deferred benefits.

A Quick Review

- Are you ready for an estate plan? Do you know what information you'll need?
- Is it important to you that your desires will be carried out as you wish? That is the goal of estate planning — to shelter your assets from taxes and to have your plans carried out as you wished.
- Have you determined which of your beneficiaries will receive what assets? How do you plan to determine that?
- Do you know the difference between wills and trusts?
- If you already have an estate plan in place, when is the last time you reviewed it?
- Have you had a life-changing event, such as a stroke or other health problem? Have you come into more money? If so, have you reviewed your estate plan to determine if it covers any of these changes?
- Is a 529 plan the best method for you to help a younger family member with college?

Chapter 11:

Ending Thoughts

The Caboose

I hope that this book is helpful to you. My purpose here is to give you all the tools and information you need to work hand in hand with your financial advisor to create a retirement investment plan that meets your needs now and in the future.

Investing and planning is all about comfort. With the right plan and knowledge, you can feel much more secure about that "good life" Tony Bennett sings about. If you're comfortable with what is happening with your money, then you have little or no fear in this major portion of your life!

Because money is a means to help you enjoy life and a way to take care of those you love, it's important you seek the best advice. I'm proud of our accomplishments at Georgetown Capital Group, and many investors see fit to allow us to advise them. If you already have your retirement portfolios with GCG, I thank you for your confidence and trust. If you are considering becoming a member of our investment family, I hope this book has been of assistance to you, and that you'll strongly consider coming in or calling so we can set up a review of your assets.

I believe in the saying, "anything is possible." Don't fall victim to thinking that there are very few avenues available to you when it comes to aiming for the type of retirement you want. But there's no time to waste, regardless of your age. Please use the notes section at the end of this chapter to jot down some thoughts about your retirement, then see a financial planner for advice.

About Georgetown Capital Group

Georgetown Capital Group was founded in May 1987. The firm has grown and flourished in more than fifteen years. Today, Georgetown Capital Group manages nearly $400 million dollars in investments in more than 14,000 accounts for more than 4,000 clients.

Georgetown Capital Group's principal and advisors are separately registered representatives of the independent broker-dealer Royal Alliance Associates, Inc. In this capacity the group consistently ranks in the Top 15 offices of the more than 500 offices of Royal Alliance Associates, Inc.

Georgetown Capital Group has some of the most sophisticated investment analysis software available, which includes the use of the principles of Modern Portfolio Theory, which won its researchers the Nobel Prize for Economics.

The staff includes eleven licensed professionals with the average advisor having more than fiftteen years in the financial arena. In addition to a Certified Fund Specialist, advisors have concentrations in life insurance, estate planning, small pension planning for schools, hospitals and other non-profit organizations, providing answers to most any question.

Investment-savvy clients stay with Georgetown Capital Group for the long term, and our clients are some of the best people I know. We provide them the finest personal service and the knowledge that their business is truly appreciated.

And many of the accounts at Georgetown Capital Group range in the quarter-million dollar and above category — clients that often are ignored by some of the larger, more impersonal firms.

Important Consumer Information

A broker-dealer "BD", investment advisor "IA", a BD agent, or IA Representative may only transact business in a state if first registered in that state, or is excluded or exempt from registration in that state as a broker-dealer, investment advisor, BD agent or IA Representative, as appropriate. Follow-up, individualized responses to persons in a state by such a firm or individual that involve either affecting or attempting to affect transactions in securities, or the rendering of personalized investment advice for compensation, will not be made without first complying with appropriate registration requirements, or an applicable exemption or exclusion.

For information concerning the licensing status or disciplinary history of a broker-dealer, investment advisor, BD agent, or IA rep, a consumer should contact his or her state securities law administrator.

NOTES

NOTES

NOTES

Glossary

A

Accrued interest — The interest due on a bond since the last interest payment was made. The buyer of the bond pays the market price plus accrued interest.

Acquisition — The acquiring of control of one corporation by another. In "unfriendly" takeover attempts, the potential buying company may offer a price well above current market values, new securities and other inducements to stockholders. The management of the subject company might ask for a better price or try to join up with a third company.

American Stock Exchange (AMEX) — The second largest stock exchange in the United States, located in the financial district of New York City. (Formerly known as the Curb Exchange from its origin on a Manhattan street.)

Amortization — Accounting for expenses or charges as applicable rather than as paid. Includes such practices as depreciation, depletion, write-off of intangibles, prepaid expenses and deferred charges.

Annual report — The formal financial statement issued yearly by a corporation. The annual report shows assets, liabilities, revenues, expenses and earnings—how the company stood at the close of the business year, how it fared profit-wise during the year, as well as other information of interest to shareowners.

Annuity — A contract by which an insurance company agrees to make regular payments to someone for life or for a fixed period.

Application — The application is a form that comes with a fund's prospectus. Investors open accounts with mutual funds by completing the application, which asks for basic information from the investor, including name, type of account, tax identification number, and service option choices. When completed, the application, along with a check made payable to the fund, is mailed to the fund company.

Assets — As an accounting or investment term, assets refer to owned items, such as cash, stock, equipment, and real estate.

B

Bear — Someone who believes the market will decline.

Bear market — A declining market.

Before-tax earned income — Income earned from your employment before you pay your taxes. It includes salaries, commissions, wages, tips, self-employment income, etc. Basically, what you get from working. It does not include income from your savings and investments (which is called unearned income).

Beneficiary — A person, organization, or trust who will receive the proceeds of a life insurance policy when the insured person dies. If you designate your spouse as the policy beneficiary, he or she will receive payment from your life insurance policy at your death.

Blue chip — A company known nationally for the quality and wide acceptance of its products or services, and for its ability to make money and pay dividends.

Bond — A bond is a contract representing the terms of borrowing and repayment for a debt. See also **Security**.

Broker — A broker, also called a Registered Representative or account executive, is a licensed person authorized to receive commissions. Brokers are always affiliated with a brokerage company, or broker-dealer. The broker-dealer is responsible for oversight of their affiliated brokers. Brokers generally work for commissions, while Registered Investment Advisors work for fees.

Bull — One who believes the market will rise.

Bull market — An advancing market.

C

Capital gain or capital loss — Profit or loss from the sale of a capital asset. The capital gains provisions of the tax law are complicated. You should consult your tax advisor for specific information.

Cash Balance Plan — A defined benefit plan in which each participant has an account that is credited with a dollar amount that resembles an employer contribution, generally determined as a percentage of pay. Each participant's account is credited with earned interest. The plan provides the benefits in the form of a lump-sum distribution or annuity.

Certificate of deposit (CD) — A money market instrument characterized by its set date of maturity and interest rate. There are two basic types of CDs: traditional and negotiable. Traditional bank CDs typically incur an early-withdrawal penalty, while negotiable CDs have secondary market liquidity with investors receiving more or less than the original amount depending on market conditions.

Commission broker — An agent who executes the public's orders for the purchase or sale of securities or commodities.

Common stock — Securities that represent an ownership interest in a corporation. If the company has also issued preferred stock, both common and preferred have ownership rights. Common stockholders assume the greater risk, but generally exercise the greater control and may gain the greater award in the form of dividends and capital appreciation. The terms common stock and capital stock are often used interchangeably when the company has no preferred stock.

D

Distribution — A distribution is a dividend payable to investors. As mentioned elsewhere, a dividend can be of three types: income, short-term capital gain, or long-term capital gain. While we're on the subject, be aware that a mutual fund dividend, or distribution, may be physically paid to the investor, or it may be reinvested in the fund, giving the investor more shares.

Diversification — Diversification refers to the numbers of securities held, and their types. For example, ten stocks would constitute a more diversified portfolio than two stocks. In addition, the concept of diversification extends beyond the confines of a single type of investment. For example, there is more diversification in a stock and bond portfolio than in a portfolio constructed entirely of stocks, alone.

Dividends — Dividends are payments made by corporations on earnings. In other words, part of the profits and income are shared with investors. This applies not only to mutual funds, but to shares of companies as well. Dividends from mutual funds may be of three types: income dividends, short-term capital gains dividends, and long-term capital gains.

E

Earnings report — A statement, also called an income statement, issued by a company showing its earnings or losses over a given period. The earnings report lists the income earned, expenses, and the net result.

EIRA — Education IRA. This account, available for the first time in 1998, allows up to $500 a year to be saved for a child's college education. Contributions are not deductible, but earnings are tax-free if used to pay college bills. Contributions depend on the contributor's adjusted gross income. No contributions can be made after the child reaches age 18.

Estate — All the assets you possess at the time of your death. These include securities, real estate, physical possessions, and cash. Your estate is distributed to your heirs according to the provisions of your will.

Estate planning — Planning to insure that your assets pass in an orderly and efficient manner to designated individuals. Estate planning includes writing wills, setting up trusts, and planning ahead to avoid unnecessary taxes.

Estate tax — The IRS fee charged in certain instances, when assets are transferred to your heirs. Estate taxes are not charged when assets are left to your spouse. When the surviving spouse dies, however, estate taxes—starting at 35% or so and reaching 55%—are levied on the value of an estate's assets.

F

401(k) Plan — A tax-deferred retirement plan that can be offered by businesses of any kind. A company's 401(k) plan can be a "cash election" profit sharing or stock bonus plan, or a salary reduction plan. A 401(k) plan carries many unique advantages for both employer and employee.

403(b) Plan – Section 403(b) of the Internal Revenue Code allows employees of public school systems and certain charitable and nonprofit organizations to establish tax-deferred retirement plans which can be funded with mutual fund shares.

Face value — The value of a bond that appears on the face of the bond, unless the value is otherwise specified by the issuing company. Face value is ordinarily the amount the issuing company promises to pay at maturity. Face value is not an indication of market value. Sometimes referred to as par value.

Financial planner — An investment professional who helps individuals set and achieve their long-term financial goals, through investments, tax planning, asset allocation, risk management, retirement planning, and estate planning.

529 Plan — Named after Section 529 of the Internal Revenue Code, a 529 plan is a type of Qualified Tuition Program that is state-sponsored, tax-advantaged and designed specifically with college savers in mind. There are two types of qualified tuition programs:

College investing plans, the more flexible of the two, allow participants to pay for tuition, room, board, equipment, and supplies at any accredited post-secondary school in the United States; prepaid tuition plans allow participants to purchase tuition credits based on their current tuition rates, usually cover tuition and fees, and are typically offered for a specific pool of participating post-secondary schools.

Flexible benefits plan —A benefits plan that allows employees to choose from a selection of taxable and non-taxable benefits, often including 401(k) contributions, health insurance, and flexible spending account contributions. Employees can elect to divert a portion of their taxable cash compensation and apply it towards qualified nontaxable benefits.

Flexible spending account (FSA) — An employee benefit that allows money to be deducted from your paycheck on a pre-tax basis, to pay for qualifying health care and dependent care expenses. A health care FSA can save you substantial sums on a wide range of medical, dental, and vision expenses that are not covered by your firm's insurance plan.

A dependent care FSA can be used to pay for childcare and eldercare costs. Contributions to your FSA accounts are exempt from federal and in some cases state income taxes. The tax exemption in effect produces "savings" of as much as 40% or more. You typically can contribute a maximum of $3,000 annually to a health care FSA and $5,000 annually to a dependent care FSA. The catch is that you forfeit any money left in your account at the end of the year, so you must carefully budget your expenses for the year.

G

Growth — Growth refers to capital appreciation. The underlying value of the investment is expected to grow. Unlike income, which is somewhat regular and consistent in most cases, growth is much less certain. However, growth investments usually outpace the returns on income-type investments over the long term (five to ten years, or longer). Growth investments usually pay little in current income.

I

Income — Income refers to the generation of regular earnings, whether from interest on bonds or from corporate dividends. Growth and income are somewhat mutually exclusive. For example, a fast-growing technology company may choose to reinvest earnings for further, rapid growth, leaving little cash for dividend distributions to shareholders.

Index — Indexes are numerical calculations, based on groups of similar investments, meant to convey the overall price level of a given market. For example, there are indexes for blue chip stocks, small stocks, foreign stocks, Treasury Bonds, and so on. Examples of indexes you may have heard of are the Dow Jones 30 Industrials, the Standard and Poor's 500 Index, the Russell 2000 index, and the MSCI EAFE (Europe, Australia, Far East) index.

Industry — Mutual funds generally are well diversified. A stock fund, for example, normally will be invested not only in a wide variety of individual stocks, but also a variety of industries, such as utilities, technology, consumer durable goods, health care, retail, and so on. Funds that focus on particular industries lack a degree of diversification, and thus are subject to increased risk.

Insurance — Insurance is a way to make an individual's financial losses more affordable by transferring them to a large group of people through an intermediary called an insurance company and a legal contract called a policy. The insurance company pools the risks of hundreds of thousands of people. The premium each policyholder pays is small compared to the potential loss he or she is insuring. The cost of a homeowner's policy, for example, is a fraction of what it would cost to replace your house if it burns down. The insurance company can afford to pay for all the losses that occur in the covered pool— and still make enough to stay in business and keep its shareholders happy— assuming; 1) that it charges appropriate premiums, and 2) that every policyholder doesn't have a loss at the same time. The larger and more diverse the pool, the less likely that is to happen.

Interest — Payments borrowers pay lenders for the use of their money. A corporation pays interest on its bonds to its bondholders.

Investment company — Investment company is another term for mutual fund. It is a company designed for investment; it is organized as a corporation, distributes shares, and pays dividends.

Issue — A security made available to the public may be called an issue. On this basis, mutual funds issue shares to investors in return for cash.

IRA — Individual retirement account. A pension plan with tax advantages. IRAs permit investment through intermediaries like mutual funds, insurance companies and banks, or directly in stocks and bonds through stockbrokers.

K

Keogh plan — Tax-advantaged personal retirement program that can be established by a self-employed individual.

L

Liability — What a person or company owes to others. The opposite of an asset.

Life insurance — A policy agreement between you and an insurance company. You agree to pay a specified amount (premium) to the company for a specified amount of coverage. Most life insurance is designed to provide funds to your heirs in the event of your death.

Load — Another word for sales charge. A load, or sales charge, is added to the net asset value of many mutual funds to come up with a public selling price. For example, if a fund's shares are worth $10, and the load is 5%, then the offering price to the public would be $10.50 ($10.00 plus 5%, or $0.50). The load, or sales charge, is paid to the selling brokerage firm, which in turn pays out much of it to the individual broker, as a commission.

Lump-sum distribution — A single payment of all your retirement money from an account, usually given when you leave a company or when you retire. Prior to retirement, lump-sum distributions are usually rolled over into another retirement plan or into an IRA. There may be tax consequences when you take a lump-sum distribution. You should consult a financial professional to discuss the taxes that may apply to any action you take with a lump-sum distribution.

M

Management — Management, or manager, is a general term that, in the mutual fund world, refers to the people who select the actual investments of a mutual fund.

Margin — The amount paid by the customer when using a broker's credit to buy or sell a security. Under Federal Reserve regulations, the initial margin requirement since 1945 has ranged from the current rate of 50% of the purchase price up to 100%.

Marking-to-Market — A process (required of mutual funds, by law) of adjusting the price of shares to a current market value, based on the value of the underlying holdings.

Maturity — The date on which a loan or bond comes due and is to be paid off.

Medicare — A government health-care plan for eligible recipients of Social Security benefits, or qualified disabled persons under the age of 65.

Money Market — Money market has come to mean a certain type of bank account (as a result of heavy marketing by bankers, of course). However, the term actually refers to debt instruments (bonds) that mature within one year. A money market mutual fund invests in money market instruments. Bonds maturing at dates greater than one year out are part of the capital market. In both cases, the terms refer to the uses to which the proceeds of the bond issues are used: as money (liquid) or for capital investment (machinery, longer-term investments).

Morningstar — Morningstar, Inc., is an investment research and information company based in Chicago, Illinois. Morningstar pioneered in-depth, timely mutual fund information service called Morningstar Mutual Funds, which has become the standard in mutual fund research in just a few years.

Mutual fund — A broad term meaning an investment company, or trust, which is owned by investors and is subject to regulations as described in the Investment Company Act of 1940.

N

NASDAQ — An automated information network that provides brokers and dealers with price quotations on securities traded over-the-counter. NASDAQ is an acronym for National Association of Securities Dealers Automated Quotations.

Net assets — When you add up the value of assets, and deduct liabilities, you arrive at the net value of assets over liabilities, or net assets.

Net asset value — In mutual fund parlance, this is the value per share. It is arrived at by taking the company's net assets, and dividing by the number of shares outstanding.

No-Load — A general term applied to mutual funds that have no sales charges or commissions.

New York Stock Exchange (NYSE) — The largest organized securities market in the United States, founded in 1792. The Exchange itself does not buy, sell, own, or set the prices of securities traded there. The prices are determined by public supply and demand. The Exchange is a non-profit corporation of 1,366 individual members, governed by a board of directors consisting of ten public representatives, ten Exchange members or allied members and a full-time chairman, executive vice chairman and president.

O

Objective — The objective of a mutual fund briefly (often in twenty-five words or less) tells what the chief goal of the fund is. For example, a fund's primary investment may be "growth with income as a secondary consideration," or "the highest level of income consistent with preservation of capital." As in food labels, the first items mentioned are usually the most important!

Offering price — The offering price is the price an investor pays per share of a mutual fund. It is the total cost per share, and may include a sales charge.

Open-End Mutual Fund — A type of mutual fund that is designed to issue and redeem shares from investors, directly, rather than through the secondary (stock) market.

P

Portfolio — A term denoting the overall collection of securities, or investments, owned by a person or company.

Pension plan — The traditional employer-sponsored pension is called a defined benefit pension plan. When you retire, you receive a predetermined benefit based on your salary and years of service. The amount is reduced if you retire before age 65. And if you are married, you will receive less because your spouse will continue to receive 50% of your pension after your death. You can get the full pension, however, if your spouse is willing to sign a waiver to his or her share. The pension replaces no more than 45% of your annual income before retirement. Since few companies give cost-of-living adjustments, your pension may seem meager by the end of your life.

A defined contribution pension plan is an employer-sponsored, tax-deferred retirement plan such as a 401(k) or 403(b). Employees elect to contribute a certain percentage of their income up to a maximum amount. Employers often match a portion of employee contributions. What you get at retirement depends on the amount you contribute, the length of time your investment grows tax-deferred, and the performance of the investments you choose.

You must contribute to get any benefit at retirement. It can take up to seven years to vest in your employer's matching funds, but you are always vested in your own contributions. When you leave the company, you can roll over the money into an IRA or your new company's plan. While a defined-contribution plan can be riskier than a traditional pension, it also has a higher potential payoff.

Principal — The person for whom a broker executes an order, or dealers buying or selling for their own accounts. The term "principal" may also refer to a person's capital or to the face amount of a bond.

Profit taking — Selling stock that has appreciated in value since purchase, in order to realize the profit. The term is often used to explain a downturn in the market following a period of rising prices.

Prospectus — The prospectus is a mutual fund's offering memorandum. It is a small booklet, generally about thirty pages long, that gives basic information designed to disclose relevant facts that investors need to make an informed decision about investing in a given fund. Federal regulations require prospectuses to cover certain basic important information, such as the fund's investment objective, expenses, management agreements, risks, and how to do business with the fund.

Q

Quote — The highest bid to buy and the lowest offer to sell a security in a given market at a given time. If you ask your financial advisor for a "quote" on a stock, he or she may come back with something like "42¼ to 42½." This means that $42.25 is the highest price any buyer wanted to pay at the time the quote was given on the floor of the exchange and that $42.50 was the lowest price that any seller would take at the same time.

R

Risk — The exposure to loss of investment as a result of changes in business conditions, domestic or foreign economies, investment markets, interest rates, relative currency rates, or inflation. Any or all of these risks may affect the market price of a security. In general, the higher the potential return on an investment, the higher the risk may be. There is generally a correlation between the amount of risk one assumes and the amount of reward one may gain as compensation for taking the added risk.

Rollover — An employee's transfer of retirement funds from one retirement plan to another plan of the same type or to an IRA without incurring a tax liability. The transfer must be made within 60 days of receiving a cash distribution. The law requires 20 percent federal income tax withholding on money eligible for rollover if it is not moved directly to the second plan or an investment company.

Roth IRA — New in 1998, this is also known as a "back-loaded" IRA. Contributions are not deductible, but withdrawals can be completely tax-free in retirement. Roth IRAs share several similarities with regular IRAs. But you can withdraw contributions at any time without tax or penalty (but withdrawals of earnings will be subject to penalties until age 59 1/2), and you do not have to take mandatory withdrawals at age 70 1/2. The unused balance on the account can also be passed tax-free to your heirs.

S

Sales charge — A commission, or extra cost, added on top of the price of a mutual fund when you buy it. The amount is calculated as a percentage of the underlying value per share. The sales charge is paid to a brokerage company, and is not invested in the fund. In other words, it is simply a cost to the investor, off the top, and is lost to the investor at the start.

SEC — The Securities and Exchange Commission, established by Congress to help protect investors. The SEC administers the Securities Act of 1933, the Securities Exchange Act of 1934, the Securities Act Amendments of 1975, the Trust Indenture Act, the Investment Company Act, the Investment Advisors Act, and the Public Utility Holding Company Act.

Sector — Sector is another word for industry. Sector funds usually focus on a single industry, such as health care, technology, or utilities. These funds are probably best avoided until investors gain a fair amount of investment expertise at a minimum. In any event, investors should endeavor to build a properly diversified portfolio before venturing into these specialty funds.

Security — A document representing participation in an investment. Stocks are securities representing ownership shares. Bonds are securities representing a contractual debt obligation of the issuer to repay the holder, with interest.

Shares — Shares are units of ownership in a corporation. For shares in a mutual fund, the ownership value of each share may be determined by dividing the net assets by the number of shares. The value of shares in a publicly traded stock is determined by supply-and-demand only, and may or not bear any discernible correlation with the value of the company's assets.

Shareholder — A mutual fund shareholder is, simply put, an investor in a fund. He or she owns shares in the fund as a result of the investment being made. Generally, shares may be purchased or redeemed for cash at any time.

Statements — Statements are periodic reports to investors regarding their investment accounts. Statements usually contain the name and address of the account holder, the date of the statement, the current number of shares, the current value per share, recent transactions that have occurred, such as purchases and dividends, and the total account value. Year-end mutual fund summaries, showing all transactions for the preceding year, should be kept by investors as long as the account is open, for tax calculation purposes, and then for a period of at least three years.

Stock — Stock is the ownership of a corporation represented by shares that are a claim on the corporation's earnings and assets. There are many kinds of stocks, the most widely known being common stock, which usually entitles a stockholder to vote in the election of directors and other corporate matters.

Stock dividend — A dividend paid in securities rather than in cash. The dividend may be additional shares of the issuing company, or in shares of another company (usually a subsidiary) held by the company.

Stock-option plan — This plan allows employees to buy a set number of shares of their company's stock at a future date and at a set price (at or below the market price at the time the option is granted) for a specified period of years. There are two types of stock options granted to employees: non-qualifying stock options and incentive stock options.

Non-qualifying stock options are employee stock options that do not meet the IRS criteria for incentive stock options and trigger a tax when they are exercised. Gains realized on the exercise of non-qualifying options are taxed as ordinary income in the year in which the options are exercised.

Incentive stock options are employee stock options that allow the employee to purchase shares of company stock under conditions that meet the IRS criteria for incentive stock options. The employee does not pay income tax when the options are granted or exercised. Profits from the sale of stock held at least two years from the date of the option grant or one year from the date of transfer to the employee are taxed as capital gains.

T

Tax deferred — An investment with earnings and sometimes contributions that are taxed at a later date. For example, you pay no taxes on your IRA's accumulated earnings until you take them out, at which time they are subject to income tax. Tax deferral gives investors a big boost because earnings compound at a faster rate than with investments that are taxed every year. Tax deferral also can cost you less if you anticipate being in a lower tax bracket when you withdraw your money, such as during retirement.

Tax-deferred annuity — An investment that postpones (but doesn't eliminate) taxes on earnings until you dip into the savings, usually for retirement. A fixed annuity pays a set amount at regular intervals. Payouts from variable annuities change because they depend on the success of the investments that make up the annuity. You usually have no restrictions on how much you can save, but you can't dip into the savings until you are 59½ years old (or else you face significant taxes, tax penalties, and penalties from the company issuing the annuity).

Ticker — A telegraphic system that continuously provides the last sale price and volume of securities transactions on exchanges. Information is either printed or displayed on a moving tape after each trade.

Trading — Trading refers to the buying and selling of investments, such as stocks and bonds, for a mutual fund.

V

Volume — The number of shares or contracts traded in a security or an entire market during a given period. Volume is usually considered on a daily basis and a daily average is computed for longer periods.

W

Will — A legal document that specifies how assets in your name only will be distributed after your death and outlines guardianship of minor children. Without one, the state in which you live will determine how the assets will be distributed. This is known as dying intestate. A will is absolutely critical for someone with chil ren.

Withdrawals — When money is withdrawn from a 401(k) plan, the withdrawal is referred to as a distribution. 401(k) plan assets can be withdrawn without penalty after age 59½. Employees are required to begin taking distributions after age 70½.

Y

Yield — Also known as return. The dividends or interest paid by a company expressed as a percentage of the current price. A stock with a current market value of $40 a share paying dividends at the rate of $3.20 is said to return 8% ($3.20÷$40.00). The current yield on a bond is figured the same way.

Yield to maturity — The yield of a bond to maturity takes into account the price discount from or premium over the face amount. It is greater than the current yield when the bond is selling at a discount, and less than the current yield when the bond is selling at a premium.

Joseph V. Curatolo
President and Owner of Georgetown Capital Group, Inc.

About the Author

Joseph V. Curatolo, president and owner of Georgetown Capital Group, is a visionary. Shortly after graduating from the University of Buffalo in 1976 with a degree in management, he entered the financial industry knowing it would be where he would make his mark.

Carving out his niche didn't take long. By 1980, Mr. Curatolo became the largest producer of tax-free securities in the country for his employer. Shortly after that, he became a branch manager of Sherwood Capital Group.

In early 1987, he left that company to form Georgetown Capital Group because he had a burning desire to run a firm where each client received individual investment attention to help their portfolios grow. He believed that if the money of his top 150 clients kept growing, they would refer him to others and his business would expand.

Six months after opening the firm, Mr. Curatolo faced an immediate crisis, the October 1987 stock market crash. However, because of portfolio positioning and individual attention, not a single client left the firm, a claim few companies can make. Now, twenty-five years and almost one hundred awards after entering the financial industry, his investment expertise has helped thousands of clients plan to become financially secure.

Mr. Curatolo's insights are highly regarded in the national investment community. He regularly meets with managers of some of the largest mutual funds in the nation. He was a three-year member of the twelve-person Royal Alliance Associates, Inc. Advisor Panel, and was a member of Putnam Fund's National Advisor Council for five years. He has just been appointed to a six-member national panel for Liberty Investments. Microsoft's msn.com registered him on their list of recommended financial advisors.

However, the most important honor he received may have been the 1999 DALBAR Financial Professional Seal. It's a national award that recognizes financial professionals who have exceeded national benchmarks in areas of trust satisfaction, quality of advice, financial results, and a clear regulatory record.

In addition, he is only one of ten people inducted into the Royal Alliance Associates Hall of Fame for his lifetime achievements in the field of investing.

Mr. Curatolo's specialty is individual and pension assets, advising on investments with growth potential that offer income and provide an inflation hedge. He holds General Securities Licenses Series #7 and #24, as well as a New York State Insurance License. He is a member of the International Association of Financial Planners, and in 1991 was listed in "Who's Who of Young Rising Americans in Business."